CÉZANNE

4

5

CÉZANNE

Maria Teresa Benedetti

CRESCENT BOOKS
NEW YORK • AVENEL, NEW JERSEY

Translated by Richard Pierce

This 1995 edition published by Crescent Books, distributed by
Random House Value Publishing, Inc.,
40 Engelhard Avenue, Avenel, New Jersey 07001

Random House
New York • Toronto • London • Sydney • Auckland

ISBN 0-517-14063-2

A CIP catalog record for this book is available from the
Library of Congress

Printed and bound in Spain by Artes Gráficas Toledo
D.L.TO:466-1995

10 9 8 7 6 5 4 3 2 1

CONTENTS

PREFACE

Paul Cézanne is a mythical figure in contemporary culture. He is
considered the father of the most important manifestations of modern art
– the revolutionary avant-garde styles as well as the quest for continuity
expressed by grafting the new onto the body of great artistic tradition.
Although much has been written about Cézanne, he is still somewhat
mysterious. This study considers both his life and works with the aim
of revealing his tormented personality, which was deeply rooted in his
childhood experiences, nurtured by solitude, and given over to radical
expressive choices that were governed by the imperative need explore his
inner being. Particular attention has been paid here to his early works,
which were connected to certain obsessions and overwrought states of mind
and which until fairly recently have been overlooked for the most part,
despite their rough-hewn, enigmatic beauty, complex psychological
implications, and crude and powerful handling that enhances the material
properties of painting.
Gradually his inner turmoil abated and his emotional power found new
outlets. His style took a new turn: it was more disciplined, based more on
observation and objective analysis than on his imagination, while
retaining the overwhelming energy of his preceding works. This was the
period, from 1872 to 1877, of his working companionship with 'the humble
and colossal Pissarro,' of his belief in the penetrating power of outdoor
painting, and of his discovery of the intimate fascination of nature
through colour. Cézanne sublimated his rage and opened his heart and
mind to natural beauty, embarking on the monumental task of reshaping
Impressionist pictorial procedure.
He soon had to address the problem of meditating on and organizing
his sensations so as to grasp their essential qualities. He assimilated the
Impressionist discovery of light and colour but, unlike his fellow artists,
he was searching for permanence and did not strive to capture mere
atmospheric effects and the fleeting moment.
Cézanne returned to Provence and became intimate with its nature, whose
austere beauty corresponded perfectly to his temperament. The strong light
there heightened the volume of objects, thus contributing to his ever
growing need for logical and orderly structure. He carefully selected his
motifs, since he wanted to find those that would best allow him to render
the immutable aspects of nature. On the one hand he lent greater clarity
to volume and on the other he integrated the different pictorial elements
into a transcending unity that represents the complexity of the universe.
Cézanne thus achieved a 'harmony parallel to nature' and transformed
common objects into universal symbols.
The artist's almost compulsive insistence on executing the same motif
again and again manifests his inexhaustible creativity. Certain late works
clearly reveal a tendency to render the disintegration of the image
– something quite unusual in an artist like Cézanne who was so strongly
attached to solid structure and consistency, but certainly no less
fascinating. The object, which until then had been characterized by its
rigorously self-contained volume, once again became receptive to the
vibrations of atmosphere and seemed to share the artist's suffering and
creative torment. Mont Sainte-Victoire, the mountain of Cézanne's youth,
became the symbol of a non-existent place, a mirage, a sublime utopia,
while the portraits of the old gardener Vallier are a sort spiritual testament
that seek to become part of the rhythm of the universe.

Maria Teresa Benedetti

THE QUEST FOR THE ABSOLUTE

The Early Years

♦ Photograph (c. 1900) of the road to Le Tholonet, with Mont Sainte-Victoire in the background. A fundamental part of Cézanne's oeuvre, this massive cone can be seen in all directions from Aix-en-Provence and the surrounding countryside.

Three boys shared their sentiments and experiences at Aix-en-Provence: Paul Cézanne, Émile Zola and Baptistin Baille. They fed upon poetry, fiery romantic visions, and the intense sensations that nature aroused in them. Theirs was a passionate bond of friendship which, together with their common and deep love of their native countryside, would later manifest itself in Cézanne's artistic vision in his final years, which revolved around a nostalgia for idyllic natural beauty and the memory of a past male *camaraderie*. The trio took long swims in swiftly running streams, caught fish with their hands, ran madly through the countryside, and hiked to the top of the gray and stone-covered Mont Sainte-Victoire which dominated the Tholonet valley, or to the Pilon du Roi, a peak near the small town of Gardanne. They wrote passionate poetry, talked about unrequited romantic love and dreamt of an adventurous, glorious future. "Do you remember the pine that grew on the side of the Arc [River] and leant its bushy head out over the chasm yawning at its feet? This pine that protected our bodies from the burning sun with its needles, ah! may the gods preserve it from the deadly blows of the woodcutter's ax!" Cézanne and Baille wrote to Zola in 1858, regretting the absence of their 'poetic, Bacchic, erotic, fantastic, old' friend who had gone to Paris. In another letter written the following year, Cézanne drew the three lads bathing in the shade of a large tree; this was one of his first drawings.

In the mid-19th century Aix-en-Provence was a peaceful provincial town rich in beautiful churches and old houses built of warm-coloured stone. It was surrounded by hills and vineyards dominated by the massive Sainte-Victoire at the foot of which, near the Bibémus rock quarry, was a dam designed by François Zola, Émile's father, an engineer who died prematurely in 1847, leaving his project unfinished.

Émile and Paul met in 1852 in the courtyard of the Collège Bourbon. Cézanne was thirteen and Zola a year younger. Though they were quite different in character, they were "attracted to each other by secret

♦ Paul Cézanne, Bathing, 20 June 1859. This pen drawing was part of a letter Cézanne sent to Émile Zola, his childhood friend, with whom he shared adventures, dreams of glory and ideals well into their twenties.

♦ The nature of Provence, the contrasts and play of light created by the intense sunlight on the thick maquis vegetation, were a constant source of inspiration and motifs for Cézanne.

10

affinities, the as yet vague torment of a common ambition, the awakening of a superior intelligence," as Zola later recalled. Born in Paris, the future writer lived in straitened circumstances, while Cézanne was the son of a rich banker, Louis-Auguste, who had come from a village in the Var region, became a successful hat dealer and exporter in Aix and later bought the only bank in town, which took on the name of Cézanne & Cabassol. In 1844 Louis-Auguste married Anne-Élisabeth-Honorine Aubert after they had already had two children, Paul and Marie, while another girl, Rose, was born in 1854. Paul, Émile and Baille, who later became head of an optical instruments industry, alternated sports with a passion for literature and poetry. Zola wrote verses that he read to his friends, who also wrote poems, and the three played music, made chemical experiments, wrote plays in rhyme and translated the Latin poets. In later correspondence, Cézanne's translation of Vergil's II *Eclogue* – '*trahit sua quemque voluptas*' – bore witness to his lasting bucolic feeling. The artist's youth was strongly influenced by literature, the effect of which lasted throughout his life. The first fruit of this passion was the poem *Une terrible histoire* (A Terrible Story) that Cézanne wrote and sent to Zola in December 1858; it began as a parody that soon became a fervently erotic tale.
Although he was physically strong, Cézanne was much more delicate on an emotional and psychological level than his buddies, often prone to fits of depression, his mind beclouded by 'demons.' The passion for painting had not yet fully taken hold over him, though in 1859 he received a prize at the municipal drawing school at Aix, where he frequented lessons held by

♦ *Paul Cézanne,* View of the Colosseum in Rome, after F.-M. Granet, *1863-65. Painted in reverse with respect to the original, this view of the Colosseum,*

purchased by the French state and in the Louvre since 1806, was perhaps an homage to François-Marie Granet, the most important painter in Aix at the time.

♦ *Les Infernets, near Le Tholonet, one of the places where Cézanne, Zola and Baille spent the long summer days in 1859. The artist portrayed his friends as 'brigands,' declaimed verses of Musset and seemed to be full of* joie de vivre. *Cézanne later told Joaquim Gasquet: "We*

serenaded the local girls [...] Listen, I played the cornet and Zola, who was more distinguished, the clarinet [...] What cacophony! But the acacias wept on the walls, the moon made the portal of St.-Jean Church azure and we were fifteen [...] At that time we thought we had the world in our grasp!"

Joseph-Marie Gibert, who was also a curator at the local art Museum. What the school offered was rather uninspired; lessons consisted of the usual life classes, figure studies, drawing mouldings, copying sentimental lithographs and painting in oils. Direct contact with nature was not part of the programme, despite the fact that the Aix Museum had some fine plein-air studies by François-Marie Granet.
The Aix Museum had no contemporary paintings to speak of, with the exception of a large painting by Ingres, *Jupiter and Thetis*. The French government's policy regarding encouraging the fine arts consisted in sending off to the provinces the mediocre works that had been purchased at the Salons; consequently, the Aix-en-Provence Museum acquired vapid paintings by second-rate artists such as Édouard-Louis Dubufe and Félix-Nicolas Frillie that Cézanne dutifully copied.
In February 1858 Zola had to go to Paris to be with his mother, and this was a disturbing factor in his friendship with Cézanne; their correspondence shows that they both suffered from this separation. The letters range from merriness to melancholy, from vitality to despondency. "Are you swimming? Are you going on sprees? Are you painting? Are you playing the horn? Are you writing poetry? In sum, what are you doing?" They praised each other's efforts, challenged each other and were at one in their fits of sadness, sexual frustration and love fantasies. They dreamed of working together and sharing glory. Cézanne was becoming more and more attracted to painting, while Zola dreamed of becoming a writer. "I had a dream the other day. I had written a beautiful book, a wonderful book, which you had illustrated with beautiful, wonderful pictures. Both our names shone in gold letters on the title page and, inseparable in this fraternity of genius, passed on to posterity."

The Decision to Become a Painter

After passing his baccalaureate exams, Cézanne enrolled in law school at the University of Aix in the autumn of 1858, while continuing his creative studies and activities. All his life he would be influenced by his classical formation; even though he tirelessly sought to create a new painting style, at heart he was a humanist who loved to read.
His passion for painting became ever more urgent and the following summer Paul took along his box of

paints on his excursions with his friends; at Les Infernets, between the dam and Sainte-Victoire, Zola and Baille posed for the painting *The Brigands*. In his first novel, *Claude's Confession* (1865), Zola described the last summer the three friends spent together in Provence: "[...] We dreamed of love and glory [...] With a sense of the richness of my soul I liked the idea of poverty [...] Because of your ignorance of reality, you seemed to believe that the artist, in his sleepless nights, earns the morrow's bread."
At first Cézanne's father opposed his son's resolve to become a painter but in the end relented. He felt that success was based on wealth and now despaired of his son's acquiring the social acceptance that had eluded him,

♦ *Paul Cézanne,* Landscape with Fisherman, *1860-61. This is one of Cézanne's first*

paintings, which reveals romantic elements and a link with academic procedures.

as he was considered a parvenu.
In 1859 the banker bought the Jas de Bouffan, a large estate with an 18th-century manor only two kilometers from Aix that had once been the residence of the Governor of Provence, in order to enhance the good name of his family. In vain: the local society continued to ostracize Cézanne *père* after a fashion, thus aggravating Paul's introspective tendencies and his difficulty in communicating. The Jas de Bouffan was to become a basic part of Paul's career: the large manor, the rows of chestnut trees, the pool with its dolphin and lion sculptures, the farm, and the low walls can be seen in many of his works.
In the salon Paul painted a mural

of a fishing scene at twilight, a combination of romantic elements and conventional painting; he transformed the decoration of another wall by representing a male nude similar to Courbet's *Bather* rendered in a picturesque manner. From 1860 to 1862 he painted four panels in the alcove of the salon, the four seasons, executed with light colours and elegance that are a conscious allusion to classical models. With a touch of irony and facetiousness that masked his vulnerability, Cézanne signed the panels with the name of Ingres and dated one – *Winter* – '1811.' He later added another work in the style of Lancret and in the center set a portrait of his father.

In this period of prolonged creative adolescence Cézanne manifested a romantic spirit that he continuously repressed and then reasserted. His passionate reactions to every circumstance had one common denominator – intensity. By now totally taken up by art, he not only worked in Gibert's classes but painted outdoors as well. He was supported by his mother, who stated: "What

♦ *Early 20th-century photograph of the Jas de Bouffan manor house, which played an important role in Cézanne's life. He painted the house in different, sometimes quite distant, periods of his production and was especially fond of the rows of chestnut trees and the pool, which can be seen in many of his canvases.*

♦ *The panels of the* Seasons *that Cézanne painted in the alcove of the Jas de Bouffan salon. These are supposed to be his first works, but considering the colour scheme and clarity of draughtsmanship, they seem to be a somewhat facetious attempt to recreate the spirit of Renaissance allegorical painting.*

The Salon des Refusés

In 1863 the jury selection of the works to be exhibited at the Salon – the biennial art show held at the Palais de l'Industrie – was particularly severe. Three-quarters of the 5,000 works submitted by 3,000 artists were rejected. This aroused an outcry, especially amongst the younger generation, and in order to qualm this generalized protest the emperor Napoleon III emitted a decree on April 24, authorizing the exhibition of the rejected works in another part of the same building.

In the same year in which Delacroix died, Manet, who as Zacharie Astruc said, represented "the glow, inspiration, strong flavour, and surpise of this Salon," found himself in the middle of a furious debate. The newspapers printed the hostile reaction to the new art on the part of both critics and public: the middle class was still bound to conventional, academic art; the avant-garde artists were repudiated, while those who painted historical or mythological subjects in an insipid, ingratiating "official" style were well received.

The scandal revolved around Manet's *Déjeuner sur l'herbe*, which was ridiculed for the brutal realism of its subject, the fact that the female nude was not idealized and the lack of narrative elements. Perhaps this work would not have attracted such hostility had it not been structured by means of frank, accentuated contrasts in such an audacious, straightforward manner. Its supposed vulgarity lay not only in the subject, but also in Manet's rejection of the traditional smooth brushwork, his application of flat colour, his summarily wrought details and

♦ *Édouard Manet,* Le déjeuner sur l'herbe, 1863;. *Oil on canvas, 208 × 264 cm (81 7/8 × 104 in). Musée d'Orsay, Paris.*

background, the forms created through colour and not line, or at most, by sketching the contours with thick brushstrokes that modelled the volumes instead of delimiting them.

The striking difference between his style and that of the historical, allegorical painting based on polished technique and conventional prettiness led the public to believe that Manet had no mastery of painting procedure. Even the presumed banality of the subject was criticized, and only many years later was Manet found to have based his composition on an engraving after Raphael and to have been inspired by Titian's (or Giorgione's) *Fête champêtre* at the Louvre.

Although he himself believed in the bourgeois ideals of the time, Manet was not accepted by his class, while he stirred enthusiasm among the new generation of painters, including Cézanne and Zola. The former admired the work because it represented a new conception of art and an innovative technique. The latter, aroused by the ridicule heaped on Manet's canvas, was led to study the artist's proud protest against academic prejudices; three years later he wrote an impassioned attack against the Salon juries that laid bare their behind-the-scenes abuses and intrigues.

12

♦ *Photograph of Cézanne in 1861. Using this as a model, the 22 year-old painted a somber, almost sinister self-portrait with an intense, brooding look.*

♦ Christ in Limbo *and* Mary Magdalene, *c. 1867. Painted for the Jas de Bouffan, this canvas drew inspiration from Italian Renaissance painting. It was later cut into two pieces; the right-hand one is in the Musée d'Orsay, Paris, and despite the cut maintains its formal balance.* Mary Magdalene *was most probably taken from Domenico Fetti's* Melancholy *kept in the Louvre.*

do you expect? His name is Paul, like Veronese or Rubens!"
Towards the end of April 1861 Paul began his Parisian adventure, which at the outset was anything but happy. He attended the Académie Suisse, an art school with life classes, and went to the large museums – the Louvre, Luxembourg Palace, Versailles. His opinion of the painters at the Salon was rather inconsistent: he was attracted by Meissonier, Cabanel and Doré, precisely those artists that were the target of the new generation's criticism. But when he saw Caravaggio and Velázquez at the Louvre he understood the difference between these masters and the obscure Baroque painters in the churches at Aix. This discovery may have brought about that mood of anxiety that made him think himself incapable of painting. Tormented by this depression, he threatened to return

to Aix to become a bank clerk. He did a portrait of Zola, threw it away, and began another one. "Paul may have the genius of a great painter, but he'll never have the genius to become one. The slightest obstacle makes him despair," his friend said. Among the various portraits of Zola, there is a chiaroscuro sketch with the author in profile that is then used in the female figure at the far right of *The Temptation of St. Anthony* (1870). Cézanne's unsettled state of mind is clearly seen in a self-portrait that was almost certainly taken from a photograph, in which he attempts to change the general effect while retaining the details; he lengthens the face and accentuates the cheeks, chin and eyebrows. The portrait thus takes on a rather menacing character of rebellion against others – but especially against his own self. As Lawrence Gowing says, this sombre

and surprising canvas with its metallic grey tones betrays the gloomy mood and dream-like despair that seems to accompany the artist in this period. Cézanne was dejected, full of doubts, and no longer in harmony with Zola, who was more and more caught up in his projects, so in September he decided to return to Aix. This was the first manifestation of his difficult relationship with Paris; his sojourns in the capital would alternate with longer and longer periods spent in his beloved Provence. For a short period he worked in his father's bank, but he soon enrolled again in the local art school and at the end of the year was back in Paris. He painted a view of the dam (which Zola's father had designed) in memory of the long excursions he had made with his friend on the Tholonet road, when they skirted the Château Noir estate and then crossed the Domaine St. Joseph, which at that time belonged to the Jesuits, who offered the boys hospitality.

♦ *The rows of chestnut trees at the Jas de Bouffan. Almost a symbol of the changing seasons, these magnificent trees were an ideal backdrop for Cézanne's meditation on nature. The large manor house, which was sold in 1898 after the death of the artist's mother, was an integral part of Cézanne's personality and art.*

♦ *The* Château Noir, *with Sainte-Victoire in the background. In a sort of spatial-temporal cycle, the sites of Cézanne's youth, of his carefree outings with his friends Zola and Baille, are the same in which he returned to live in the latter part of his life.*

In Paris and Aix-en-Provence

In the early 1860s the artistic life in Paris was brimming with vitality. Although the Salon and the École des Beaux-Arts were dominated by the proponents of insipid academic classicism, the young painters drew inspiration from the innovative realism, which had introduced a taste for nature, a new receptive approach to landscape, a sense of humanity, and a technical audacity that stressed brushwork, tone and texture. In his *Salons* (1846-1859), Baudelaire had clearly expressed the features of art that captured the dignity and beauty of contemporary reality. And in his *The Painter of Modern Life*, dedicated to Constantin Guys, he says: "Modernity is that which is transient, fleeting, contingent: one half art, the other half eternal and inimitable."
Great Spanish painting was seen and admired in the Louvre exhibition of

brushstrokes. Though he admired Manet, who had revealed a refined and virtuosistic painterly technique, a new means of applying colour, Cézanne preferred thick texture, similar to that of the Provençal painter Monticelli with his Daumier-like touch; the budding artist was especially attracted to the latter's palette in the style of Delacroix. A mixture of impetuosity, rage and eroticism betrayed his sexual frustration, which gave rise to volcanic and disagreeable compositions. His reserved nature and provincial status certainly did not help his social life, and he often masked his uneasiness and timidity behind coarse behaviour. Zola, who championed naturalism, was less appreciative of Cézanne's gloomy works, as he preferred the canvases of the future Impressionists – Pissarro, Monet, Degas and Renoir, who were involved in the 1863 Salon

were marked by sensuality and violence, yet contained a well-balanced and calculated chromatic rendering which, as Roger Fry says, evinces a sensitivity to colour influenced by Delacroix. This was the art of a solitary and irascible soul, art that was apparently instinctive and was yet highly elaborated, with a thick texture that bore witness to his boundless inner torment. The works of this period reveal Cézanne's introverted character, his family problems and his difficulty in mastering painting technique. While the future Impressionists were representing the light of Île-de-France, Cézanne was seeking darkness in canvases of death and crime in which feeling often took on the guise of grief, love and fury were inseparable, and the whole was dominated by eccentric, and at times grotesque, inspiration – a world that bore the stamp of turbulence and macabre poetry. These compositions often lacked in verisimilitude and show that he was tackling technical problems that for the moment were beyond him;

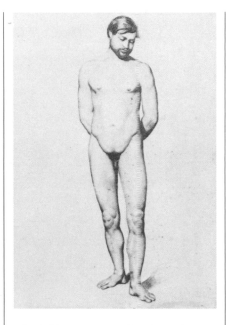

♦ *Paul Cézanne,* Male Nude, *1862. Pencil, 61 × 47 cm (24 × 18 1/2 in). Musée Granet, Aix-en-Provence. The artist executed this* *drawing at the municipal drawing school in Aix. It reveals a mastery of academic technique and a delicate touch.*

Louis Philippe's collection; Japanese prints had become quite popular. When Cézanne returned to Paris, he found a new artistic climate. After being rejected at the École des Beaux-Arts he went back to the Académie Suisse, where he met Pissarro, who had noticed the 'strange Provençal' whose drawings from life, derided by everyone, reminded him of Veronese. Pissarro was the first person to recognize the young artist's unique personality, and they became fast friends. Cézanne discovered the female nude, which unsettled and intimidated him, as he confessed in his letters to Zola.
His canvases gave vent to obsessive fantasies; the gloomy motifs were translated violently, with broad

des Refusés, which made Cézanne determined to side with the new anti-academic naturalistic painting that drew inspiration from real life. He often returned to Aix, but even in Paris frequented his Provençal friends – Baille, Numa Coste, the sculptor Philippe Solari, the painter Achille Emperaire, the writers Anthony Valabrègue and Paul Alexis, and Antoine-Fortuné Marion, a scientist and amateur painter. He became more intimate with Pissarro and Guillaumin, who loved to find fantastic titles for his canvases. When he was in Aix, Paul shut himself up at the Jas de Bouffan, where he did portraits of his father, his sisters and friends, and his uncle Dominique Aubert. From 1863 to 1870 most of his works

♦ *Paul Cézanne,* Man Lying on the Ground, *1862-65. Black crayon, 22 × 29 cm (8 5/8 × 11 3/8 in). Museum Boymans-van* Beuningen, *Rotterdam. This drawing with its free-style composition is among the first Cézanne did during his stay in Paris.*

the figures are out of proportion and the compositions are dominated by groups set in the foreground. Vivacity and solemnity alternate, carefully arranged landscapes represent adolescent emotions, and still lifes rendered with vigorous brushstrokes pursue a majestic balance.
The portraits are in the style of Courbet, not only in their size and execution, but also in their approach to the model. However, they are strongly individual works which show that the artist lacked only experience in order to exploit his artistic gifts to the full. Besides the fine portrait *The Artist's Father* (1866), there is the *Self-portrait* executed the same year in which he models his head only by means of colour and his high forehead, beard and forceful look create the image of an inspired artist.

♦ *Paul Cézanne,* Bather on the Rocks, *1860-62. Chrysler Norfolk Museum (Virginia). This male nude, modelled after Courbet's famous* Bather, *once decorated the left-hand wall of the Jas de Bouffan salon before Cézanne put his four panels of the* Seasons *there.*

13

The thick layers of paint betray Cézanne's urgent striving after mastery of the organization of space and volume, even at this early stage. During this period his conception of art as intense and powerful feeling and his conviction that greatness lay in extremism, produced works that seem to be forerunners of Expressionism; yet when he managed to channel the intensity of his imagination into the study of nature he produced fine works. In the summer of 1865 Cézanne attended the art school, had long discussions with his friends, and listened to music, expressing his admiration for Wagner, which inspired

14

The Café Guerbois Group

♦ *Henri Fantin-Latour*, Studio in the Batignolles Quarter, *1870. Oil on canvas,*   *204 × 273.5 cm (80 × 107 5/8 in). Musée d'Orsay, Paris.*

"Nothing could have been more stimulating," Monet noted, referring to the group of artists that met at the Café Guerbois in the Batignolles quarter of Paris in the late 1860s, "than the regular discussions we used to have there, with their constant clashes of opinion. They kept our wits sharpened and supplied us with a stock of enthusiasm which lasted us for weeks, and kept us going until the final realization of an idea was accomplished. From them we emerged with a stronger determination and with our thoughts clearer and more sharply defined."

Manet was the recognized 'leader' of the group of habitués: the poet and sculptor Zacharie Astruc, the writer Edmond Duranty, the critic Armand Silvestre, the painters Antoine Guillemet and Frédéric Bazille and the engraver Félix Bracquemond. Often others took part: Fantin-Latour, Degas and Renoir, as well as Zola, the musician Edmond Maître and Constanin Guys. Cézanne, Sisley, Monet and Pissarro went to the café occasionally, when they were in Paris; and the photographer journalist and caricaturist Nadar, famous for his aerial photographs of Paris taken from a hot balloon, was a sometime visitor.

Here there was a noisy, animated atmosphere marked by a keen ambition for success, an adversity to prejudice, an anti-conformist stance and the desire to prove the validity of the new artistic ideas through the new paintings. The discussions often became quite heated; one altercation between Manet and Duranty led to a duel, which fortunately had no consequences; and Manet and Degas often had rows.

A cultured bourgeois who was ambitious and impulsive despite his good nature, Manet did not agree with those artists who sought a new style completely divorced from tradition and museums. Degas, who was often isolated in this group, put his talent for intelligent irony to good use, and it was hard to argue with him. He had no use for social problems, and was opposed by Pissarro and Monet. While Degas and Manet represented the well-educated, well-to-do bourgeoisie, the others had a humbler social status. Though his family was rich, Cézanne expressed his contempt for convention with his rude manners, intolerance for the opinion of others and gruff taciturnity. Zola on the contrary was a gifted talker and took an active part in the discussions. Though worn out by his struggle to eke out a living, Monet was an attentive listener, while Renoir expounded the need for artistic maturity through contact with the great works of the past, and argued with those who claimed that studying nature was sufficient.

In spite of its different ideas and characters, the Café Guerbois group was united in its contempt for academic art and the desire to seek artistic truth outside of conventional procedures. In 1870 Fantin-Latour painted a portrait of the group, with Manet seated at his easel surrounded by the German painter Scholderer, Renoir, Astruc, Zola, Maître, Bazille, Monet.

his *Overture to Tannhäuser*. In February 1866, back in Paris, he was again with Zola and the other friends with whom he shared projects and dreams. Solari had exuberant visions, Zola was reviewing books for "L'Événement," and Cézanne was preparing canvases for the upcoming Salon, proud of the fact that they would never be accepted and animated by the desire to challenge the jury. He had been rejected at the 1865 Salon, which was marked by the scandal caused by Manet's *Olympia*, and his canvases met the same fate the following year, despite the fact that Daubigny, a member of the jury together with Corot, defended him. He decided to write a letter to the Count de Nieuwerkerke, the Director of Fine Arts, requesting that the Salon des Refusés be revived. As he received no reply, on April 19 he wrote a second letter in which he stated: "I cannot accept the unfair judgement of colleagues who I myself have not expressly asked to appraise me." These very ideas were again expressed by Zola a short time later in his articles in "L'Événement." Having obtained permission to review the Salon, Zola violently attacked the jury and revealed how it got itself elected, stating that any unorthodox, innovative artist was bound to be rejected. Using the pseudonym 'Claude,' Zola expounded aesthetic theories that were the fruit of long

♦ *Henri Fantin-Latour*, Tannhäuser: Venusberg, *1864. County Museum of Art, Los Angeles. The Paris premiere of Wagner's opera took place in 1861, causing a scandal amongst the conservatives. Tannhäuser,*   *the medieval hero reinterpreted in a romantic key, inspired several artists: besides his homage* Overture to Tannhäuser, *Cézanne utilized the atmosphere of the opera in* The Temptation of St. Anthony.

discussions with Cézanne. He attacked the 'daubers painting for amusement and vanity,' the painters who ignored nature and the hostile, prejudiced public – all of whom stifled the emergence of 'works alive and human, full of deep truth and interest.' Because of the readers' protests, Zola was forced to discontinue his series of articles, which he reprinted in a pamphlet entitled *Mon Salon*; it was

♦ *Marie Cézanne, the elder of Paul's two sisters, in a photograph taken in 1861 when she was twenty. A devout*   *Catholic and spinster, she was instrumental in her brother's religious conversion at the end of the century.*

published in the spring of 1866 and contained a long dedication to Cézanne. But it was really the friend of his youth he was addressing rather than the young artist: "It is for you alone that I write these few pages, I know you will read them with your heart, and that tomorrow you will love me more affectionately [...] Happy are they who have memories! I envisage

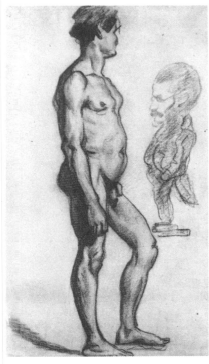

♦ *Paul Cézanne, Male Nude, 1863-66. Charcoal, 50 × 30 cm (19 11/16 × 11 13/16 in). Private Collection. This drawing, probably executed in the Académie Suisse,* dates from Cézanne's second sojourn in Paris. He went to the academy every day except Sunday, from eight to one and then from seven to ten in the evening.

your role in my life as that of the pale young man of whom Musset speaks. You are my whole youth; I find you mixed up with all my joys, with all my sufferings. Our minds, in brotherhood, have developed side by side. Today, at the beginning, we have faith in ourselves because we have penetrated our hearts and flesh."

According to Monet, Cézanne had the habit of placing a black hat and a white handkerchief near the model he was painting in order to establish the two poles between which he would settle the tonal values. At the time he was not particularly fond of painting directly from nature, and his works were a combination of the monumental power of Courbet and the influence of the Spanish masters he so admired. Unlike Manet, Cézanne did not draw inspiration from Velázquez or Goya, but preferred dramatic effects in the style of Zurbarán and Ribera. Although he spoke of the usefulness and beauty of plein-air painting, he himself did not yet work directly from nature, since at the time he was more receptive to striking clashes of colour. His still lifes and portraits had greater tonal simplification, a bolder technique and more forceful colour contrasts than those by Monet and Manet.

The character of the painter Claude Lantier in Zola's novel *Le ventre de Paris* (1873) was based on Cézanne: "[...] about thirty, bearded, with knotty joints and a strong head. A very delicate nose hidden in his moustache, eyes narrow and clear [...] deep in his eyes, great tenderness." Then, while writing *L'Œuvre*, which was published in 1886, he recalled how wary of women his friend was, and dwelt on Cézanne's deliberately coarse language. Joaquim Gasquet, who met the artist towards the end

of his life, gives an even more vivid description of his suffering, isolation and despair: "[...] those combinations of violence and timidity, of humility and pride, of doubts and dogmatic assertions which shook him all his life. He would shut himself up for weeks, not wanting to let a living soul enter his studio, shunning any new acquaintance." A studio in utter disarray, where he worked doggedly. The avant-garde intellectuals and artists acknowledged Manet as the leader of their group, which often met at the Café Guerbois in the Batignolles quarter. Cézanne took pleasure in displaying rude manners and would exaggerate his Provençal accent almost as if in defiance of the refined mannerisms of his colleagues, Manet in particular. Although he admired Manet, he disapproved of what he considered his bourgeois stance. Not content with showing his contempt for conventions in his painting, he wanted to express this revolt in his behaviour as well. As Monet later recalled, he would enter the café and cast a mistrustful look at the group. He would then open his waistcoat, pull up his pants and, with a flourish, adjust

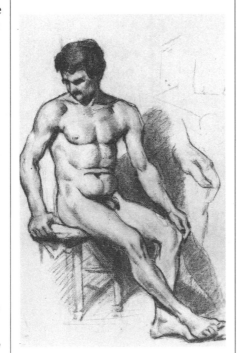

♦ *Paul Cézanne, Seated Male Model, 1865-67. Charcoal, 25 × 32.3 cm (9 7/8 × 12 3/4 in). Art Institute of Chicago. The Académie Suisse was a* private art school in which artists could paint from live models for a modest fee and which had neither teachers nor examinations.

Zola as an Art Critic

♦ *Paul Cézanne, Portrait of Émile Zola, 1862-64. Oil on canvas, 26 × 21 cm (10 1/4 × 8 1/4 in). Whereabouts unknown.*

Zola became interested in art even before Cézanne went to Paris; after having visited the Salon des Refusés he supported the avant-garde movement. Through Cézanne he met Pissarro and Guillemet, with whom he discussed the works of Manet, to whom he dedicated a laudatory article in 1867. In 1866 he became the critic for the daily newspaper "L'Événement," where he expounded his idea of a work of art as 'a corner of nature seen through a temperament,' underlining the specific importance of this aspect. He stated that his fondness for an artist like Courbet lay not so much in his social principles as in the energy with which he rendered nature. He was convinced that an artist is not such because of the subjects he depicts, but for what he is. "Genius consists in rendering an object or a person in a new way, thus making them truer and greater. As for me, I am not moved by the representation of a tree, a face or a scene, but by the man whom I find in the work, the powerful individuality he has created therein, next to God's world, a world all his own that my eyes will never forget."

Seeing that a new edition of the Salon des Refusés was out of the question, Zola wrote a series of combative articles in 1866; the first two concerned the Salon jury and its illicit method of having itself elected, and another was an homage to Manet, who had been rejected from the latest Salon.

In another article, Zola tackled the problem of realism, stating that the subject was subordinate to the personal way it was handled. Because of the many letters of protest, the owners of the newspaper were forced to ask Zola to stop writing art criticism. Zola wrote two more arti-

cles in which he attacked some artists and lauded others such as Corot, Daubigny and Pissarro. However, Cézanne is never mentioned, as Zola thought his friend had not yet fulfilled his promise. In his articles on *Naturalism at the Salon* published in 1880 for "Le Voltaire," though he defended the Impressionists, he expressed ideas that contrasted with their artistic vision and criticized the way they had handled their public image. He reproached them for having refused to submit works to the Salon, taking as an example Manet, whose obstinacy had been rewarded, and stated that the Impressionist exhibitions were failures despite the large public they had attracted in those years.

In May 1896, he once again played the role of art critic, this time for "Le Figaro." His review of the Salon revealed how distant he then was from Impressionism. "Suddenly the Salon of thirty years ago came back to me. And what a heartthrob [...] I was twenty-six. I was then intoxicated with youth, with truth and the intensity of art, drunk with the need of asserting my beliefs with knockdown blows." But he could not help remarking on the 'insanity to which the theory of reflected light' had led: "[...] really disconcerting works, these multicoloured women, these violet landscapes and orange houses which are being given us with scientific explanations that they are like that as a result of a certain reflection or decomposition of the solar spectrum." He deplored the 'futility of discussions, of formulas and schools' and was repulsed by the exaggeration and ugliness of the works themselves. Van Gogh stated that Zola's knowledge of painting was insufficient and expressed prejudice rather than 'just judgement.'

his red sash, after which he would shake hands with everyone. Everyone except Manet, who was reserved special treatment. Cézanne would take off his hat and in a nasal voice say with a smile: "I will not shake your hand, Monsieur Manet; I have not washed for a week." He would then sit by himself in a corner, apparently indifferent to the conversation. But sometimes, when someone expressed an opinion that was opposed to his own, he would stand up abruptly and go out without uttering a word.
At the 1867 Salon the works presented by Cézanne were the object of many curious comments as well as an article by a certain Arnold Mortier that was reprinted in April in "Le Figaro": Mortier spoke of two rejected paintings by a certain 'Sésame,' the same person "who, in 1863, caused general mirth in the Salon des Refusés

by a canvas depicting two pig's feet in the form of a cross." Zola immediately wrote a letter of protest, calling his friend "a young painter whose strong and individual talent I respect extremely." Cézanne was more interested in laying bare the incompetence and hostility of the Salon jury than in being accepted.
In 1868 he was again rejected, while works by Manet (including *Portrait of Émile Zola*), Pissarro, Bazille, Monet and Renoir were exhibited.

The Vanguard Versus Tradition

Zola's reviews in "L'Événement" became less aggressive and offered a carefully thought-out analysis of modern landscape. "The classical landscape is dead, killed by life and by truth. No one nowadays would dare to say that nature needs to be idealized, that the sky and water are vulgar, and that it is necessary to make horizons harmonious and correct in order to create beautiful works." He defended a truthful interpretation of nature in original language on the part of painters who retain their individuality and humanity. He also stated that it

was necessary to paint entirely outdoors. Boudin and Monet had already begun plein-air painting, and Pissarro had sent landscapes to the Salon (now kept at the Hermitage Museum) that were executed *sur le motif* (directly on the spot). Cézanne rarely worked outdoors in this period, despite what he said to Zola in 1866: "You know, all pictures painted inside, in the studio, will never be as good as the things done in the open air. When outdoor scenes are represented, the contrast between the figures and the ground is astounding and the landscape is magnificent." These opinions were then reflected in Zola's writings, in which Cézanne's works are never mentioned, despite the fundamental role he played amongst the artists rejected by the Salon. The reason may lie in the fact that Cézanne was Zola's closest

childhood friend, but his artistic friendship with other painters, in particular Manet, was more important at this time: Manet's œuvre and prestige could contribute to the future success of Zola's theories and this artist represented the counterpart of his ideas on naturalism. Even though some common friends felt that Cézanne was a greater artist, Zola did not support him because, despite his faith in his friend's genius, he doubted he would ever be able to express it. A letter he wrote to the critic Duret, who had asked Zola to introduce him to Cézanne, is quite significant in this regard: "Wait until he has found himself."
In fact, Cézanne had not yet broken free from his turbulent imagination which conditioned his work on both a thematic and formal level. Thanks to Courbet's influence, the others curbed their imagination through direct experience, but Cézanne felt he was a visionary. One of the most impressive canvases of this period, *The Rape* (or *The Abduction*, 1867), was executed in Zola's house in Rue de la Condamine and Cézanne gave it to his friend.
A curiously tanned giant is carrying

in his arms a pale female figure with blue-black hair. The relationship between her white flesh and his bronze skin is violent and is further accentuated by the blue-green background of the landscape. Zola later mentioned this in *L'Œuvre*, showing his admiration for its bright colour scheme, dramatic composition, powerful expression and the marked individualism of the companion of his childhood.
In this phase of his career Cézanne's canvases are often quite different both in technique and composition. The size varied, and some scenes were totally imaginary, while in others he adopted sketches he had executed at the Académie Suisse. Valabrègue said: "Every time he paints one of his friends, it seems as though he were revenging himself on him for some hidden offence."

♦ *Paul Cézanne, Factories at L'Estaque, 1869. Cézanne Studio, Aix-en-Provence. This watercolour, which the artist did to decorate the cover of Zola's* / *mother's workbox, is a rare, and certainly not complimentary, homage to industry – the only time Cézanne's realism coincided with Zola's.*

♦ *Published by an unidentified Paris daily newspaper, this biting caricature by Stock shows Cézanne with the two paintings of* / *his that were rejected by the 1870 Salon: the sad Portrait of Achille Emperaire and an unidentified reclining female nude.*

LE SALON PAR STOCK

♦ *Paul Cézanne, Man's Head, 1867-70. Charcoal, 30 × 23 cm (11 7/8 × 9 in). Private Collection, Paris. This drawing, contemporaneous to* / *the extraordinary charcoal portraits of Achille Emperaire that were studies for Cézanne's much derided 1870 oil portrait, shows how much progress the artist had made.*

In the works he executed outdoors he applied the paint vigorously with the palette knife in order to lend emphasis to the landscape. "You are perfectly right," he said to Pissarro, "to speak of grey, for grey alone reigns in nature, but it is terrifyingly hard to catch." He painted the Jas de Bouffan garden or the banks of the Arc River, with a palette in which he juxtaposed white, blue, green and black. He realized he could obtain grey through colour, but it took him years, and above all the example set by Pissarro, to discover the possibility of rendering a vast range of tones in all their richness by means of the technique of applying dabs with his brush.
In Paris at the beginning of 1869 he met Hortense Fiquet, a 19 year-old model from the Jura region. She was a tall, lovely, brunette with a sallow complexion and large black eyes. Cézanne, who was eleven years older than Hortense, fell in love with her and persuaded her to live with him, keeping this a secret from his parents. Neither his art or his relationship with his friends seems to have been affected by this new state of affairs in his emotional life.
In 1870 the Salon jury once again rejected the two paintings Cézanne had submitted. The critics' ferocious remarks were aimed especially at *Portrait of Achille Emperaire*, a large, strange canvas that was also caricatured by Stock. Despite these disappointments, his paintings took on new power and boldness and the development of his art was to a certain extent linked to the experiments of his early career.

Cézanne and Impressionism

In July 1870 Cézanne, wanted by the police because he had not responded to the call-up during the Franco-Prussian War, was living with Hortense at L'Estaque, a village near Marseilles. "I divided my time between landscape painting and working in the studio," he later told the art dealer Vollard. The war had scattered the group of artists: Pissarro and Monet were in London, while Renoir, Manet and Bazille were in the army; Bazille was killed on November 20 during the attack at Beaume-la-Rolande. Cézanne had just emerged from a depressing and intense period spent at Aix that is reflected in a work, *Pastoral* (or *Idyll*), in which three female nudes probably embodying sensual passion surround a bearded man (who is obviously Cézanne himself) reclining on the bank of a river amidst vegetation with clearly phallic overtones. This tone of sexual fantasizing is seen in canvases inspired by Flaubert such as *The Temptation of St. Anthony* and *The Feast*; other works seem to be styled after Manet: *Le Déjeuner sur l'Herbe*

♦ *Paul Cézanne (middle) with Camille Pissarro (right) in Auvers-sur-Oise around 1874. His older friend converted him to plein-air painting, and Cézanne spent two years – which were crucial to his artistic development – between Pontoise, where a small group of painters gathered around Pissarro, and Auvers. Cézanne later confided to Émile Bernard: "My youth was filled with*

passionate canvases in which I drew inspiration in turn from Veronese, Ribera, Caravaggio, Courbet and Delacroix. Only when I met Monet and Pissarro, who had already freed themselves from such impediments, did I understand that one must draw from the past only in order to learn how to paint [...] In the old masters they were seeking only the colour, which would give rise to a new use of the palette."

♦ *Cézanne looking for a motif outdoors in the Auvers region (c. 1874). In this village he was able*

to work undisturbed both on the road that led to Dr. Gachet's house and in the open country.

(1870-71) and *A Modern Olympia* (1869-70). These new allegorical subjects can be linked to his life with Hortense, which marked a release from his sexual tension and lent greater audacity and sincerity to his works. One cannot ignore the allegorical representations of his state of mind; compared to Manet's and Zola's production, his works are marked by deeply rooted conflicts, some of an erotic nature. His still lifes, beginning with the splendid and mysterious *Still Life with a Black Clock* (c. 1870), now played a leading role in his conception and rendering of his subjects. At L'Estaque Cézanne worked outdoors, where he did landscapes without human figures in impasto or executed with the palette-knife technique that had much in common with his preceding 'black' canvases: the same passion and vigour, the same violent colour contrasts. Even the most commonplace motif was dramatized. He was inspired by the bay of Marseilles surrounded by mountains, and painted the village roofs, the chimneys that rise up towards a cloudless sky, the pines on the green hillsides, the distant reflections of the rocky islets on the water. The study of nature became fundamental to Cézanne's art. The style of his youth was destined to make way for a new-found serenity and humility; having discovered the 'natural motif,' the contents of his poetic world took on original forms. At the end of the war the Café

Guerbois group reunited, now gathering in the Café de la Nouvelle-Athènes. Cézanne was not at Aix when the Third Republic was proclaimed and he was nominated member of the local art school and Museum committee. After Hortense gave birth to their son Paul on 4 January 1872, Cézanne went with his family to stay with the Pissarros at Pontoise. Pissarro, the doyen of the Impressionists, who with his sincere and vigorous personality was able 'to transform art into pure, eternal truth' (as Zola said), wanted to expose his younger friend to the experience of plein-air painting. His role as friend, adviser, teacher and companion in artistic adventures, added another fundamental dimension to his position

17

♦ *Paul Cézanne, Portrait of Camille Pissarro, c. 1873. Pencil, 10 × 8 cm (3 7/8 × 3 1/8 in). Cabinet des Dessins, Musée du Louvre, Paris. Speaking of Pissarro's role in*

his life, Cézanne said in 1902: "As for the old Pissarro, he was like a father for me, a man who gave precious advice, something similar to the Good Lord."

as an artist. 'The humble and colossal Pissarro,' as Cézanne called him, was a paternal and tutelary figure who embodied the quest for truth and new pictorial techniques. Hence his charisma amongst the Impressionists, some of whom stayed with him at Pontoise. Pissarro followed Cézanne's progress, stating that he would 'astonish a lot of artists who were too hasty in condemning him.' From the time they had met ten years earlier he had had faith in his artistic qualities and was now happy to see Cézanne dominate his unstable temperament in his new intimate contact with nature. For his part, Cézanne was quick to recognize his friend's positive influence; he copied one of Pissarro's views of Louveciennes, assimilating his mentor's brushwork, replacing modelling with the building up of tones and brightening his palette. Like

18

♦ *Paul Cézanne,*
Portrait of Dr.
Gachet, 1872-74.
Département des
Arts Graphiques,
Musée du Louvre,
Paris. Paul Gachet
was a friend of
the Café Guerbois
artists and
frequently took part

in their meetings.
His features are
familiar to us
because of Van
Gogh's famous
portrait of 1890 in
the Musée d'Orsay
in Paris. Gachet
took care of the
Dutch artist in the
last years of his life.

♦ *Paul Cézanne,*
Snow Effect, Rue
de la Citadelle,
Pontoise, 1873.
Oil on canvas,
38 × 43.6 cm (15
× 18 1/8 in). This
canvas disappeared

during World War
II, probably in 1944
during the pillage
of the Château de
Rastignac in
Dordogne on the
part of the German
army.

Monet and Renoir, who often painted the same motif, Cézanne and Pissarro began to work together. "We often set up our easels side by side, but it was certain that each of us kept the one thing that counts, his own 'sensations'. Pissarro later acknowledged being influenced by his friend while at the same time having influenced him. Pissarro's approach to nature was essentially a humble one that allowed him to penetrate her, and Cézanne's devotion and receptivity to nature were unparalleled. Daubigny, one of the Barbizon painters closest to Impressionism, lived in the nearby village of Auvers-sur-Oise, where Dr. Paul Gachet, a habitué of the Batignolles group meetings, had bought a large house that overlooked the valley. As he was an amateur engraver, Gachet invited Pissarro, Guillaumin and Cézanne to do etchings, putting his plates and press at their disposal. In early 1873 Cézanne moved to Auvers, where he took up residence near Gachet; here he executed his only etchings and many still lifes, especially of the lovely flowers Mme. Gachet picked and placed in Delft vases for him. Auvers was a tiny village of little houses with thatched roofs and earthen paths; Cézanne painted the road leading to the Gachets' house and the open fields. He worked slowly, returning to the same spot twice in the same day, "once for cloudy weather and once for sun; many a time he would struggle desperately with a canvas, working on it in different seasons, and even different years, so that a spring scene painted in 1873 would end up becoming a snowy landscape in 1874," as Gachet later said.

His palette became lighter and he began to use long, supple palette knives that allowed him to paint large

areas of colour, capture the essential features of the motif and heighten the shadows, lending a certain plasticity to the scenes of nature. Although he adopted Pissarro's technique of summary brushstrokes, in many canvases he applied thick layers of colour produced by daubs and spots in order to render every nuance. He worked slowly and patiently, yet this procedure in no way eliminated spontaneity. His impressions were so strong, he was so determined

♦ *Camille Pissarro,*
Portrait of Paul
Cézanne, c. 1874.
Pencil, 19.4 × 11.1
cm (10 5/8 × 4 3/8
in). Cabinet des
Dessins, Musée du
Louvre, Paris.
Pissarro wrote the
following about
Cézanne's
production in this

period to the critic
and art collector
Théodore Duret,
who was interested
only in original
talent: "You will like
Cézanne, since he
has done some
particularly strange
studies and some
truly unique
landscapes."

to penetrate nature's secrets and so humble in his attempts to fix his sensations, that not even the heavy building up of colour and thick texture could destroy the sincerity and power of his perceptivity. He followed Pissarro's advice and utilized 'the three primary colours and their immediate derivatives,' and his paintings of winter scenes and the effect of melting snow led him to brighten his palette even more to obtain a light grey.

*P*issarro's Influence

Cézanne's decision to work on landscapes was the result of a process that led him to prefer Aix and Provence, or Pontoise and Auvers, to Paris. His single-minded, violent and yet pathetic revolt against social conventions and his inability to adapt to bourgeois behaviour fit in well with Pissarro's revolutionary spirit and the

anarchic side of his temperament. Pissarro advised Cézanne to find the aspects of nature which corresponded to his own temperament, to render the subject through forms and colours rather than through drawing. Form could be achieved by means of "the brushstroke, the right shade of colour and the correct degree of brightness." The elder artist also told his friend to render sensations in the most direct fashion by choosing the suitable technical means, while the eye must try to take in everything by painting without hesitation in order not to lose the first impression. Pissarro also insisted that nature was the artist's master. Consequently, Cézanne learned to observe and render the myriad effects of light on the same motif. He adopted an aerial perspective that lent overall unity to his canvases and created uniform atmosphere with colour. He proceeded quite slowly, as if he were working on a mosaic. One day in the outskirts of Auvers a peasant happened to see him at his easel, which was rather distant from Pissarro's, and he said to the latter: "Well, boss, you have an assistant over there who isn't doing a stroke of work!"

Though Cézanne's works were somewhat similar to those of the Impressionists, they differed in his insistence on a calculated inner structure. He began to develop the method of applying paint characteristic of his so-called constructive period as well as a new and brighter palette; yet he had to work very hard in order to obtain Delacroix's rich colour, which he admired so much and which he derived from nature. He was aware of Pissarro's aversion to museums and his desire to "portray what we see and forget what appeared before our time." He studied the effects of light and air and sought to render them through colour; he also saw that objects have no specific colour of their own but reflect one another and that light comes into play between the observer's gaze and the object. Lucien Pissarro, the artist's eldest son, recalled how at this time Cézanne began to construct the surface of his canvases by means of subtly applied diagonal brushstrokes, whereas his father painted in comma-like strokes. By applying colour in short parallel strokes he brought together the various objects in a tautly woven texture and overall unity of colour. When he was asked why he had abandoned the fervour so characteristic of his first period and now adopted the technique of separate touches, Cézanne said:

♦ *Paul Cézanne, Pissarro Going off to Paint, 1874-77. Pencil, 20 × 11 cm (7 7/8 × 4 1/3 in). Cabinet des Dessins, Musée du Louvre, Paris. The following is from a letter Cézanne wrote to Pissarro on 2 July 1876: "There are subjects that would require three or four months' work and that could be found, since the vegetation doesn't change here. The olive and pine trees always keep their leaves [...] The sun here is so tremendous that it seems to me as if the objects were silhouetted not only in black and white but in blue, red, brown and violet. I may be mistaken, but this seems to be the opposite of modelling."*

♦ *Photograph of Cézanne around 1875. "If the eyes of people around here could cast deadly arrows, I would have been done for long ago. They don't like my looks." (Letter to Camille Pissaro, 2 July 1876.)*

"I cannot convey my sensation immediately; so I put colour on again, and I keep putting it on as best I can. But when I begin, I always try to paint sweepingly, like Manet, by giving form with the brush." Consequently Cézanne's paintings are amazingly rich in colour; he would place many small daubs on the first layer of paint, thus lending extraordinary chromatic effects. There is a great range of colour in all the objects on the canvas. The sky abounds with nuances, as do the straw roofs, the trunks of trees and their foliage; even the outlines of objects undergo the same careful and loving treatment, as they are rendered in blue, yellow and maroon. Cézanne stated that there are no lines in nature, no shadows without colour. Much later in his career he said that pure drawing is an abstraction and that there is no distinction between drawing and outline, "since everything in nature has colour."

However, by employing this technique, Cézanne found it difficult to finish a painting. When Gachet noted that his friend risked compromising a canvas by continuing to apply paint, he persuaded him to stop; and Cézanne would obey, albeit unwillingly. Gachet purchased many works by Cézanne, Pissarro and Guillaumin, and the grocer in Pontoise accepted some paintings as payment of his bills. Cézanne had not yet abandoned agitated fantasy scenes; he finished another *Temptation of St. Anthony* as well as *A Modern Olympia* (1873), which is perhaps the strangest work he executed in Auvers. He worked at a feverish pace and was reluctant to be separated from Hortense and their son for any length of time, and was also afraid his father might cut off his allowance if he learned about their relationship. When his parents insisted he go back to Aix, he begged off, stating that it would be all the more

difficult for him to leave them if he had to return to Paris at a moment's notice. Cézanne asked his father for 200 francs a month in order to be able to work in a place that offered so many opportunities for his painting. Pissarro and Gachet's warm friendship injected confidence and a feeling of optimism in him. The former introduced him to Durand-Ruel, the first art dealer to support Impressionist artists, who ended up bankrupt but succeeded nonetheless in making their works known. Cézanne also met Père (Julien) Tanguy, a paint merchant who had been a travelling salesman, then had fought with the Paris Commune militia, was captured and sent into exile, and after being released opened his shop in Rue Clauzel in Montmartre, becoming a staunch supporter of the Batignolles group. He appreciated Cézanne's works and gave him painting materials in exchange for his canvases.
The 1873 Salon once again went badly for the Batignolles friends, and the art

♦ *Paul Cézanne, House and Tree, 1873-74. Oil on canvas, 65 × 54 cm (25 1/2 × 21 1/4 in). Private Collection. "I begin to find myself superior to those around me, and you know that the good opinion I have of myself has only been reached after mature consideration. I must always work, but not to achieve a final polish, which is for the admiration of imbeciles." (Letter to his mother, 26 September 1874.)*

critics of the new Republic proved to be no more receptive than those in the Second Empire. Courbet was rejected because he had openly supported the Commune and Monet, Pissarro and Sisley refused to submit their works in protest. On the other hand, Manet's *Le Bon Bock*, a relatively modest canvas influenced by 17th-century Dutch genre painting, was a great success. These artists became increasingly convinced of the need to free themselves from the prejudiced, all-powerful Salon juries by forming an independent corporation and exhibiting their works on their own. Paul Alexis declared: "While having no desire to seem to be a prophet, I foresee the artistic success of a generation of radicals – I refuse to use the vague term 'realists' – who are children of modern science, lovers of truth and experimental precision, who reject conventional beauty, the classic ideal and romantic poses and whose sole banner is that of sincerity and life." Cézanne must have been pleased to hear what Alexis stated the day of the Salon inauguration: "A jury cannot but be ignorant and blind. Instead of attacking it, which serves no purpose, we are ready to abolish it."
On 15 April 1874 the exhibition of the Société Anonyme des Artistes, Peintres, Sculpteurs et Graveurs was inaugurated in Nadar's studio in Boulevard des Capucines. Pissarro had persuaded Cézanne to submit three canvases: two landscapes of Auvers and *A Modern Olympia* (which Gachet had lent him). This first public 'trial' of the new artists was marked by difficulties, the public was disoriented and the critics at odds.

20

The First Impressionist Exhibitions

♦ *Paul Cézanne,* Portrait of the Artist Guillaumin, *1870-72. Pencil and crayon, 23 × 17 cm (9 × 6 5/8 in). Museum Boymans-van Beuningen, Rotterdam.*

Thirty artists are listed in the catalogue of the first Impressionist exhibition, which was held in Nadar's studio on the Boulevard des Capucines on 15 April 1874. Among them were Boudin, Degas, Guillaumin, Monet, Morisot, Pissarro, Renoir, Sisley and Cézanne. It seems that some members of the group were afraid that Cézanne's canvases might cause a public outcry, but Pissarro and probably Monet insisted that he be allowed to participate. Just as occurred in the Salon des Refusés, the public reacted quite negatively, aided in this by reactionary critics. The review in "Le Rappel," for example, said that no jury, not even in a dream, would accept works by Cézanne, a painter "who came to the Salon carrying his canvases on his back, like Jesus Christ carrying the cross. An over-exclusive love of yellow has compromised Cézanne's future up to now." One of the most derided canvases was his *A Modern Olympia*, which was executed in 1873 at Avers-sur-Oise and belonged to Gachet. "On Sunday the public saw fit to sneer at a fantastic figure that is revealed under an opium sky to a drug addict [...] M. Cézanne merely gives the impression of being a sort of madman who paints in delirium tremens," stated a woman journalist who used the pseudonym of Marc de Montifaud. The other artists were also the butt of cruel comments, the most famous example being that of Louis Leroy, who in "Charivari" derisively coined the term 'Impressionism' upon seeing Monet's famous *Impression, Sunrise* – a name destined to become a household word.

The second exhibition in 1876 was, like the first, inaugurated a month after the Salon, in the Durand-Ruel gallery. It basically presented the same artists, with the exception of Cézanne, who had returned to Aix. This time there was mixed criticism, as Théodore Duret and Edmond Duranty supported the Impressionists. The latter, a friend of Degas, wrote in *La nouvelle peinture* that the real discovery of this group "consists in the realization that a strong light discolours tones, that sunshine, reflected off objects, tends by virtue of its clarity to blend its seven prismatic rays into a single, uncoloured brilliance which is light." Monet, who sold a canvas for 200 francs, planned a third exhibition for the following year with the help of Durand-Ruel and Gustave Caillebotte, the young painter and art collector who was only too ready to help out his friends financially.

The third Impressionist exhibition opened in April 1877 in an apartment on the rue Le Peletier. Monet exhibited no fewer than 30 canvases, and Cézanne's 17 works were hung in the most prominent position in the main room. Georges Rivière, who had replaced Zola as art critic, published a short work, *L'Impressionniste*, for the exhibition, stating that the Impressionists differed from the others because they handled subjects as colour rather than as the subjects themselves. He praised his friends in his articles and called Cézanne "the artist who has been the most attacked, the most mistreated by the press and public for the past fifteen years." He recognized Cézanne's greatness: "Those who have never wielded a paintbrush or a pencil have said he did not know how to draw and they have reproached him for imperfections which are in fact subtle refinements achieved through enormous skill."

♦ *Paul Cézanne,* The Artist's Son, *c. 1878. Pencil, 10.8 × 7.3 cm (4 1/4 × 2 7/8 in). Private Collection, Paris. For over five years Cézanne managed to keep his liaison* with Hortense, and the existence of his son, a secret from his father. The latter found out about this situation in 1878, when he opened a letter to Paul from Victor Choquet.

♦ *Paul Cézanne,* The House of the Hanged Man, *c. 1873. Oil on canvas, 55 × 66 cm (21 5/8 × 26 in). Musée d'Orsay, Paris. This is one of the last works Cézanne executed at Auvers before returning to Paris* in 1874, when he took part in the first Impressionist exhibition. The show was a dismal failure for him; his A Modern Olympia was attacked by the critics and derided by the public.

Leroy, the "Charivari" critic who mockingly coined the term 'Impressionism,' which caught on and was adopted by the artists themselves, called into account Corot as an accomplice to the crimes committed in his name. Other critics such as Silvestre, Burty and Castagnary recognized the talent of the painters and their original style. But Castagnary also spoke of "deplorable signs of decomposition" in Cézanne's works. *A Modern Olympia*, with its drastic treatment of the 'scandalous' motif of sensuality and corruption through extremely free handling of the subject and high-keyed tones, was a thin disguise for Cézanne's radical anti-bourgeois stance and triggered violent criticism. However, Count Doria purchased his *House of the Hanged Man*.

On the whole, the exhibition was a financial failure. Later, in *L'Œuvre*, Zola described the atmosphere, with the hostile, sneering public so typical of an avant-garde show. After the closure, Cézanne suddenly decided to return to Aix to ask his father for more money, but the latter was upset about his son's debts and lack of success. The artist was not discouraged, however; in Paris that autumn, he wrote a letter to his mother in which he declared his self-confidence, a secret but ever-present and profound part of his psychological make-up.

In 1875 Renoir, Monet and Sisley organized an auction of their works at the Hôtel Drouot; one of the collectors interested in their works was a supervisor in the customs administration, Victor Chocquet, a veritable 'talent scout' who relied solely on his own taste without any thought of making a profit. Despite his limited financial resources, he had

bought a series of fine works by Delacroix, which was one reason why Cézanne and he got along so well. Chocquet was quick to add Impressionist canvases to his collection. That same year Cézanne took up residence in the Quai d'Anjou in Paris, painting with Guillaumin scenes of the Seine and the outskirts of town. He lived in utter solitude and had few friends with whom he could share his hopes and doubts. Chocquet became an important part of his life at this stage. Despite his admiration for Monet and Renoir, he was especially enthusiastic about Cézanne's art. After being rejected once again at the 1876 Salon, the artist spent the summer at L'Estaque, where he painted a view of the bay and many portraits of Chocquet.

♦ *Paul Cézanne, Quai de Bercy – La Halle aux Vins, Paris, c. 1872. Oil on canvas, 73 × 92 cm (28 3/4 × 36 1/4 in). Private Collection. Cézanne moved to Paris with Hortense in 1871, and they lived at the Quai de Bercy in* *front of the wine market where, according to Achille Emperaire, the noise was so deafening it would wake the dead. This, and an important event in Paul's life – the birth of his son – greatly upset the artist's equilibrium.*

The Prejudiced Public

One of these portraits, shown at the third Impressionist exhibition of 1877 along with sixteen other works by Cézanne, attracted the crowd because of its strange colours. This portrait of Chocquet is clear and calm, but the blue-green reflections in the hair, certain touches of blue in the beard, the yellow and red tones of the flesh and the greenish parts around the beard and mouth, disconcerted the public. Chocquet himself patiently tried to explain to the mocking visitors

that these were reflections cast by light upon objects, and that the pink skin so typical of official portraits was a mere convention; but he failed to convince them. While the critic for "Charivari" advised his readers, especially pregnant women, not to linger before Cézanne's painting, the review in "Le Petit Parisien" admitted that this artist had a different vision of nature. Zola, while calling Cézanne "the greatest colourist of the group," adding that his works had the makings of a great artist, limited his review of his old friend's works to these few kind words. And even those critics who were beginning to understand the art of Renoir, Monet and Morisot, generally ignored Cézanne. Disappointed, the artist decided to 'work in silence' and refrain from exhibiting with his friends. However, he continued to submit works to the Salon every year, always receiving a letter of rejection, which, as he wrote to Pissarro, he found "neither new nor surprising." Cézanne thus refused to take the opportunity offered to him by his fellow artists to show his works in their collective exhibitions held from 1879 to 1882 and then again in 1886. In this period the distinguishing feature of his art was a new-found discipline: his lighter palette and organic structural logic showed he had attained artistic maturity. There was a constant psychological element that characterized his entire oeuvre – the quest for unity and clarity, in which each dissonant component was blended into a tightly woven, harmonious fabric of a superior order. Impressionist technique had helped him to select his motifs and discover the great potential of colour. After the 1877 exhibition Cézanne continued to work in the outskirts of

Paris, at Chantilly and Fontainebleau, setting up his easel on the banks of the Seine and the Marne. As Duranty wrote to Zola, he went to the tiny café in Place Pigalle dressed in his usual shabby manner. He asked Zola, who was spending the summer at L'Estaque, to pass on his letters to his mother so his father could not open them, as was his wont. However, Père Cézanne soon found out about his son's liaison. His initial reaction was to reduce his allowance, but in the end he gave him an adequate sum. Cézanne's dedication to plein-air painting after 1872 was a return to mother nature, who was both reassuring and elusive, as well as a projection towards new techniques and motifs. He utilized colour as a means of connecting and unifying disparate elements, far and near, of different consistency, thickness and surface value. The Impressionist approach transformed the objective world into a homogeneous pattern of coloured particles. But Cézanne was not satisfied with the mere impression of a vibrant atmosphere, he did not want to dissolve the world into a coloured veil. His aim was rather to establish contact with objects, to create a communion of objects within the consistency of a nature that continued to overawe him. His landscapes, including those painted under Pissarro's watchful glance, are solidly structured, they betray a permanent, deeply-rooted construction and betoken stability and duration. Already in the first Impressionist exhibition he had felt this difference between himself and the other artists; after the third show in 1877 he went his own way, painting in solitude the landscapes of his native land, free from the tumultuous artistic ambience that reigned in Paris.

♦ *Paul Cézanne, The House of Père Lacroix at Auvers, c. 1883. Oil on canvas, 61.5 × 51 cm (24 1/4 × 20 in). National Gallery of Art, Washington, DC. While the Impressionists captured the palpitating light* *and ephemeral nature of reality, Cézanne aimed at organizing its structure and form. He grasped the essential, eternal nature of reality and penetrated beneath its apparent density and mass.*

♦ *Paul Cézanne, Red Roofs, L'Estaque, 1883-85. Oil on canvas, 65 × 81 cm (25 5/8 × 31 7/8 in). Private Collection. Cézanne wrote the following to Émile Zola on 24 May 1883: "I have rented a little house and garden at L'Estaque, just above the station and at the foot of the hill where behind me rise the rocks* *and the pines. I am still busy painting, I have some beautiful viewpoints here, but they are not true motifs. Nevertheless, climbing the hills at sunset, one has a glorious view of Marseilles in the distance and the islands, the whole giving a most decorative effect when bathed in the evening light."*

The Logic of Organized Sensations

♦ *Cézanne's house at L'Estaque, near Marseilles. When the Franco-Prussian War broke out on 19 July 1870, the artist took refuge in his beloved Provence, which he would rarely leave from that time on. He lived in this house on a hill for different periods up to 1884, when he painted innovative canvases that were crucial to the history of 20th-century art, from Cubism to Art Informel.*

♦ *Paul Cézanne,* The Pool at Jas de Bouffan in Winter, *c. 1878. Oil on canvas, 52.4 × 56 cm (20 5/8 × 22 in). Private Collection. Left, photograph of the pool and chestnut trees at the Cézanne estate (c. 1935). Cézanne replaced the 'surface' of his Impressionist friends (Pissarro, Monet, Renoir) with a well-structured three-dimensional composition which, as Roger Fry says, reveals his 'vocation for architecture.' A vocation that continued to co-exist with Impressionist 'sensations' which, far from being a contradiction, was a quest for a superior unifying principle.*

After the success of *L'Assommoir,* the novel he published in 1878, Zola bought a house at Médan, in the Île de France, which soon became a focal point of social and intellectual life. At first Cézanne was often his guest there. His landscapes were set on the banks of the Seine, and with Zola's boat 'Nana' he could go to an islet and paint the château and its annexes with parallel diagonal strokes that lent inner solidity to the overall structure. It was by no means easy for such an irascible, restless, proud and touchy person as Cézanne to feel at ease in the mundane ambience at Zola's summer house, yet at first he enjoyed his sojourns there; he could see his old friends Alexis and Coste, and writers and critics such as Duret and Huysmans. He also loved to engage Zola in discussions about painting,

even though a contrast soon emerged between the writer, who had become a 'grand bourgeois' all too willing to fill his house with exotic furniture and bric-a-brac of dubious taste, and the painter with his rude and testy manners used to a simple working atmosphere and a Spartan existence. Although he was grateful to Zola for having introduced him into the *beau monde* and was happy to have resumed their intimate friendship, which was so important for him, he nonetheless felt worlds apart from that brilliant and conventional society. On the one hand he was afraid of being judged and on the other felt he was misunderstood as well as disturbed in his work. When Vollard later asked him why he and Zola had ended their friendship, Cézanne replied: "There was never a true

argument between us [...] I didn't feel at ease in a house with carpets all over, servants and 'the other one' who worked at a desk of carved wood." His sojourns at Médan produced many fine landscapes in which the artist deliberately ignored the foreground in an attempt to render reality in a compressed form.

He felt much more comfortable at Pontoise, where he returned now and again; he stayed with Pissarro and Gauguin, who was seeking guidance for his burgeoning artistic career from the older master. Cézanne painted *sur le motif* with his friend and mentor, but now the differences that separated him from Impressionism were becoming more and more obvious. He was no longer content to render the luminosity of an atmosphere, but still shared the group's struggle for recognition.

At the 1880 Salon the paintings were hung in a different manner and much space was given over to the artists exempt from jury approval; as a result the banality of many poor painters predominated and it was difficult for visitors to find the canvases they wanted to see. Though they had been accepted, Monet and Renoir protested because their paintings had been hung badly, and asked Cézanne to get Zola to intervene, which he did: a series of articles in "Le Voltaire" entitled *Naturalism at the Salon* in which he expressed his views on the Impressionists. Despite his friendly tone, certain contrasts emerged. Zola recognized these artists' courageous commitment to their art but added that their 'masterpiece' had not yet come into being. Naturalism is the art of the future, he stated, and has already conquered the field of literature, but the "true misfortune is that not one of the group has yet succeeded in putting the new formula into practice [...] All of them are forerunners. Their artist of genius has not yet been born."

In general Cézanne agreed with his friend's view; he felt he had little in common with his former companions and saw himself as a pioneer. But even concerning his old friend, Zola was rather cool: "M. Cézanne, who has the temperament of a great painter, is still

struggling with problems of technique. All in all he is closest to Courbet and Delacroix."

His frequent absences from Paris and his lack of interest in the meetings at the Nouvelle-Athènes café, set Cézanne farther and farther apart from his fellow artists and the Parisian artistic scene. When Huysmans published a book on modern art in 1883, Pissarro complained that he had not considered the importance of his friend's art. The critic replied: "Yes, he has temperament, he is an artist, but in sum, with the exception of some still lifes, the rest is, to my mind, not likely to live." An opinion shared by those in Zola's circle at Médan.

After a period spent in the Île-de-France working with Pissarro 'without much zest,' Cézanne returned to Provence in 1882 and remained there for three years. He sometimes went to Marseilles to see his friend Monticelli and they would paint in the country. He continued submitting his works to the Salon jury, either directly or

♦ *Auguste Renoir,* Portrait of Paul Cézanne, *1880. Pastel, 55.3 × 44 cm (21 1/4 × 17 5/16 in). British Railway Pension Fund, on loan to the Victoria and Albert Museum, London.*

through the good offices of Père Tanguy, but he was always rejected. At this stage, he wanted to be accepted there only in order to impress his fellow townspeople, but to achieve this he was certainly not willing to make the slightest artistic compromise. In 1879 Guillemet had tried in vain to have a canvas by Cézanne accepted. In 1882, however, he succeeded by taking advantage of the prerogative of the jury members to exhibit a work by one of their students. The work accepted – a portrait or self-portrait – went unnoticed; Cézanne had exhibited in the Salon in virtual anonymity. He still saw his friends, painted together with Renoir at L'Estaque and went to Manet's funeral in 1883; but he had left Impressionism behind him, and the movement was in a critical stage because of the differences arising among the various artists.

◾ Paul Cézanne,
Landscape with
Trees, 1885-87.
Pencil, 12 × 21 cm

(4 3/4 × 8 1/4 in).
A. Heun
Foundation, Art
Institute of Chicago.

A New Perception of Nature

Cézanne obtained an ever firmer grasp of the material substance of painting; he transformed colour into something solid, rejecting the merely atmospheric, momentary rendering of the subject. He was wary of Monet's dissolution of the image, and although he admired him ("He is nothing but an eye, but what an eye!"), Cézanne felt that observation alone was not enough and had to be accompanied by thought and logical procedure. "There are two things in a painter: the eye and the mind. The two must cooperate; both need to be trained: the eye by studying nature, the mind by an orderly, logical approach to impressions and experiences. They create the means of expression." The difference between the fleeting sensation recorded by the

Impressionists and Cézanne's perception lies in the latter's quest for total knowledge of the subject. He said he wanted "to become classical again through nature, that is to say, through sensation." Nature was the true source of art: "But one must not reproduce it, one must interpret it [...] by means of plastic equivalent and colour." Again: "[...] There are some very beautiful views here [L'Estaque]. The difficulty is to reproduce them, this isn't exactly my line. I began to see nature rather late, though this does not prevent it from being full of interest for me."
In a letter to Pissarro he expressed his intense emotion upon seeing the bay of L'Estaque: "It is like a playing card. Red roofs on the blue sea. The sun is so implacable that it seems as though the objects are silhouetted, not only in black and white, but in blue, red, brown, and violet." The intense light

of the Midi heightens and flattens the contours of objects, imparting a soft relief to them. By means of contrasting colours (blue-orange-green-ochre) he attempted not only to render light, but also a relationship between the pictorial surface and the colour values that represent space. In the many views of L'Estaque, colour became the integral part of this world of objects. Using contrasting colours to create space, Cézanne set the precision of the planes against the Impressionist transformation of masses into coloured spots. He painted the houses, roofs and farms of L'Estaque set amidst pine trees, and in the background was the sea and a patch or vast extent of sky. Having eliminated the ephemeral, he merged the changing aspects of nature, creating a new unifying principle. Cézanne did away with atmospheric values and exterior effects, however appealing these might be; he rejected everything that made Impressionist paintings a historical document of a certain epoch. His motifs were long-familiar places filled with memories;

♦ Paul Cézanne,
Mont Sainte-Victoire
near Gardanne,
1886-90. Oil on
canvas, 62.5 × 91
cm (24 5/8 × 35 7/8
in). National
Gallery of Art,
Washington, DC.
This painting
marks a return to
one of the artist's

favourite motifs,
which would
dominate the
canvases in the
years immediately
following. Cézanne
seems to have come
to terms with his
temperament and to
have found inner
peace and harmony
with nature.

♦ Paul Cézanne,
Plates with Apples
and Pears, 1885-87.
Oil on canvas,
44 × 58 cm
(17 5/16 × 22 7/8
in). Metropolitan
Museum of Art, New
York. According to
Cézanne, sensory

experiences had to
be guided, as it
were; the artist
discovered partial
truths with his eyes
and then used his
mind to coordinate
the whole and effect
a definitive, overall
synthesis.

he had no desire to represent change, but sought to capture the eternal structure of reality.
In early 1885 his solitary contemplation of nature was interrupted by a violent and mysterious love affair with a woman about whom very little is known, except that she and Cézanne had met in Aix. An unfinished love letter on the back of a drawing only partially explains this strange episode. He asked Zola to deliver their secret correspondence: "I am either mad or very sensible." To which he added a quotation from his beloved Vergil: "*Trahit sua quemque voluptas*" (Each of us is carried away by his own desires). But the following month he was at La Roche-Guyon with Renoir, and it appears that his new love was already a thing of the past. He was restless and went to see Zola at Médan. Then he went back to Jas de Bouffan. What happened after his return to Aix is not known, but a few days later he wrote to Zola: "For myself there is only absolute isolation, the town brothel or something of the sort, nothing else. I'll pay. It's an ugly

24

word, but I need peace, and I can get it, at that price. If only my family were not so meddlesome, everything would have been fine."

Every morning he went to the quaint town of Gardanne and returned to Jas in the evening. His life was anything but peaceful, as his relationship with Hortense was tense and there was no longer understanding between them. His portraits of her are eloquent in this regard: she is an extraneous being, a patient model and nothing else. And Cézanne's self-portraits betray his utter concentration on his art, the only meaningful aspect of a life that was a failure where human relationships were concerned.

He rented an apartment at Gardanne and moved there with Hortense and their thirteen year-old son, the only person with whom he had a serene and trusting relationship. The surrounding countryside, as he said to Chocquet, had not yet found "an interpreter worthy of the richness it harbours." Nestling against a hill with a church on its top, the town had a pyramid shape: roofs and square houses, the towers of the three mills, surrounded by undulating plains that stretched to the Mont du Cengle, a foothill of Mont Sainte-Victoire, the massiveness of which cut the horizon in two. Cézanne drew inspiration from this mountain, and from Gardanne he discovered its southern slope, a jagged

♦ *Paul Cézanne, Young Girl with Unbound Hair, 1873-74. Oil on canvas, 11 × 15.2 cm (4 3/8 × 6 in).*

This small canvas might be considered a preparatory study for Cézanne's compositions of bathers.

♦ *Paul Cézanne, View of L'Estaque through the Pines, 1882-83. Oil on canvas, 72.5 × 90 cm (28 1/2 × 35 7/16 in). Reader's Digest Collection, Pleasantville, N.Y. As Georges Rivière said: "The landscapes possess*

compelling majesty [...] In all his paintings the artist moves us because he himself experiences, by observing nature, a violent emotion which his craftsmanship transmits to the canvas."

plateau with bare hills and scattered dwellings in front of it. He painted this landscape with its pure forms and harmonious colours time and time again: the red of the earth, the yellow of the houses, the green of the trees. One of his favourite sites was Bellevue, a property owned by his brother-in-law Maxime Conil; it was perched on a hill with a splendid view of the valley below. Here he painted views of the house, the farmyard, the pigeon tower and the Arc River valley. Another favourite motif was a hill between Bellevue and the neighbouring property. Once again, Sainte-Victoire was in the background, which he represented in views framed by a large pine tree the branches of which seemed to fit in with the rhythm of the mountain profile. Naturally, Sainte-Victoire reaching up to the heavens took on a symbolic meaning of a quest for the absolute. In his later years Cézanne sought perfection through this sacred mountain – the profundity and solidity of nature

perceived behind the façade of an ever more extraneous human world. He loved the geological structure of his land with its broad planes, clear-cut lines, and masses that seemed to absorb all detail. He preferred the simple, harmonious lines of the sun-baked earth of Provence to the northern landscapes, as the former had more light and colour and was more contained and circumscribed. He experimented with the laws of perspective as related to colour in order to reproduce his sensations and translate the immensity and richness of nature onto a canvas. "I try to render perspective through colour alone," he said. "I proceed quite slowly, for nature reveals herself to me in very complex form." His 'strong feeling for nature' was the basis for greatness and beauty, but a knowledge of the means to express this emotion was also essential and was acquired through long experience.

As was said above, Cézanne was no longer interested in Impressionist atmospheric vibrations but sought to render the forms, colours, planes and light of a landscape. He did not share Monet's idea of representing a motif at different times of day in order to capture the varying intensity of light and was not attracted by pointillism, as Pissarro was. ("If he [Pissarro] had continued to paint as he did in 1870, he would have been the best of us all," he stated.) He felt that Manet had a poor feeling for colour and that Renoir's rendering of landscape was 'cottony.' He set himself the task of "making out of Impressionism

something solid and permanent like the art of museums." For that matter, Impressionism was passing through a crisis. The artists were rethinking their approach to artistic creation. Renoir turned to draughtsmanship, Monet to chromatic disintegration with vaguely Symbolist overtones, and Pissarro to Divisionism. The establishment of the Société des Artists Indépendants in 1884 as a 'counter-Salon' and hub of a new avant-garde movement foreshadowed the definitive break-up of the group in 1886, the date of the eighth and last Impressionist exhibition.

Monet and Renoir went to the Côte d'Azur and met Cézanne in Marseilles. Cézanne and Renoir painted Sainte-Victoire together. But the former basically kept to himself, living in virtual seclusion, continuing to work *sur le motif* at his own rhythm and discovering the profundity of reality through nature.

♦ *Paul Cézanne, Self-portrait in a White Turban, 1881-82. Oil on canvas,*

55.5 × 46 cm (21 7/8 × 18 1/8 in). Neue Pinakothek, Munich.

In the meantime, his religious sister Marie persuaded their father to consent to Paul's marriage with Hortense, after 17 years of living together; they were married on 28 April 1886 in Aix in the presence of his parents. A few months later the 88 year-old Cézanne died.

Married life did not change Paul's artistic life at all. Hortense, who did not like Provence, lived mostly in Paris with their son Paul. "She likes only Switzerland and lemonade," Cézanne once remarked, and her friends called her 'the ball,' and their son 'the little ball.' An indifferent husband, Cézanne was, however, a loving and indulgent father; after his mother died in 1897, his son became his confidant. And he gradually changed from an inveterate anti-cleric into a devout Catholic, finding support for his old age in religious faith.

The First Public Recognition

While Cézanne had enjoyed identifying himself with the main character in Zola's novel *Le ventre de Paris*, Claude Lantier, when the same person became the protagonist of *L'Œuvre* (1886) he was deeply offended and the book brought about the definitive break in their friendship. Cézanne was hurt because he thought his friend was disappointed in him and considered him an example of 'artistic impotence,' an 'abortive genius,' in short, a failure. He had already suffered because of Zola's gradual lack of enthusiasm for his art, which was partly revealed in the writer's reluctance to praise him in his reviews. His pride was wounded, because despite periods of discouragement, he believed in his talent. "My dear Émile," he wrote to Zola on 4 April 1886 after receiving a copy of the novel, "I have just received *L'Œuvre*, which you were good enough to send me. I thank the author of *Les Rougon-Macquart* for this kind token of remembrance and ask him to permit me to clasp his hand while thinking of bygone years. Ever yours under the impulse of past times, Paul Cézanne." The letter expresses significant regret for the past, no apparent interest in the present, and no hope for the future: the two would never again see each other. Zola later commented: "To start out together inspired by the same faith and enthusiasm and then to arrive alone, and reap glory by oneself, is terribly sad."

While one might ask whether Zola had acted in total good faith in writing his novel, it must be said that he had gradually moved away from his former good opinion of Impressionism and that *L'Œuvre*, which, as Alexis later said, had set out to be a study of the psychology of artistic impotence, was further proof of his lack of faith in that movement. Again, in May 1896 Zola returned to the role of art critic in a review of the Salon published in "Le Figaro" that showed how his opinion had changed and how far removed he was from his former companions. Speaking of Manet in the past, he had lauded his clear, bright painting compared to the sombre *art pompier*;

♦ *Photograph of the road to Le Tholonet with the large umbrella pines Cézanne loved to paint.*

♦ *The pigeon tower at Bellevue, near Aix-en-Provence, in a 1935 photograph. The seclusion that Cézanne loved and needed was interrupted by the occasional visit or by short periods he spent with his friends such as Renoir, who in 1889 went to live in Bellevue.*

Zola's L'Œuvre

♦ *Édouard Manet, Portrait of Émile Zola, c. 1868. Oil on canvas, 146 × 114 cm (57 1/2 × 44 7/8 in). Musée d'Orsay, Paris (gift of Mme. Zola, 1918).*

From the time he had begun the series of novels *Les Rougon-Macquart*, Zola had decided to devote one of them to the life of an artist. In Paul Alexis's book on Zola, published in 1882, the documentation was furnished by the latter, so that Alexis could announce a future project: "His chief character is [...] Claude Lantier, a painter caught up in the modern ideal of beauty who appeared briefly in *Le ventre de Paris*." According to Alexis, Zola set out to analyze the psychology of artistic impotence. "Around the central man of genius, the sublime dreamer whose production is paralyzed by an infirmity, other artists will gravitate – painters, sculptors, musicians, men of letters, a whole band of ambitious young men who have also come to conquer Paris; some of them failures, others more or less successful; all of them cases of the sickness of art, varieties of the great contemporary neurosis."

Zola intended to make this a sort of *roman à clef*. He made frequent use of personal recollections, which gave him long-needed relief after all the research he had had to make to write his previous novels. Yet though he based this novel on personal experience, using the friends of his youth as the characters, none of them is portrayed directly, and their characteristics are mixed, hence unrecognizable.

Thus Claude Lantier is not only Cézanne, but has some of Manet's traits (he is the leader of the artistic group), and his paintings reflect the artistic features of Cézanne, Manet and others. Moreover, some of Zola himself is to be found in this character.

He comes from a working-class family, that of Gervaise and Auguste Lantier in Zola's *L'Assommoir*, while his artistic formation is similar to Cézanne's, with whom Claude shares his terrible doubts and despair, his sense of failure.

Lantier's dearest friend is Sandoz, a writer that Zola uses to express his own ideas about art, "either to complement Claude or to be contrasted with him," as the author stated.

They are the main characters of the novel, the scenario of which is the Salon des Refusés, the first Impressionist exhibitions and the battles waged in support of the new art. Claude expounds certain Impressionist theories, plein-air painting, the disintegration of objects in light; but at the same time he is against hasty work, the mere sketch. Cézanne and Zola's youthful friends Paul Alexis, Anthony Valabrègue, Solari, Baille, Victor Chocquet, Cézanne's wife Hortense, and Durand-Ruel can be recognized to some degree in the secondary characters.

The final eposide of the painter committing suicide in front of a large, unfinished canvas may have been taken from Zola's having visited the study of a young artist who committed suicide in 1866 after being rejected by the Salon.

However, Claude is above all the creation of the author and the idea of artistic failure was part of Zola's general plan of a saga, a picture of a period.

George Moore rightly remarked that Zola's theory in this book was that no painter working in the modern movement had achieved what had been achieved by some writers inspired by the same ideas and aesthetic principles, thus affirming the superiority of literature over painting.

26

now he complained of "the abuse of the clear tone, which makes certain works look like laundry discoloured by extensive washing [...] And when I see this diluted, whitewashed Salon with its chalky insipidity, I almost begin to long for the black, bituminous Salons of yore." Analyzing his change of heart, Zola states that having defended avant-garde art in the past was the right thing to do, as it "represented enthusiasm and faith." But now he revolted against 'bloodless' and 'dreadful' painting that had become fashionable.
Respecting Cézanne's desire for solitude, Zola never sought him out. But when in September 1902 the artist found out his dear friend had died, asphyxiated by fumes from a chimney, he shut himself up in his studio and wept bitterly the whole day long.

*S*olitude Strengthens the Spirit

Cézanne lived in isolation and rarely saw his old friends. In 1889 Renoir rented the Bellevue estate from Cézanne's brother-in-law, and the two artists worked outdoors together in the Arc valley, setting up their easels in front of the pigeon tower. But it seems that Renoir's stay did not end peacefully; Cézanne was becoming more and more irritable because of diabetes, which grew worse from about 1890 on.
Around the end of 1894 he went to Giverny and spent a lot of time with Monet. On the latter's birthday he met Rodin, Clemenceau and Gustave Geffroy. Rodin's affectionate handshake moved him. On another occasion he met the novelist Octave Mirbeau and the American artist Mary Cassatt, who called Cézanne "one of the most liberal artists I have ever seen." Monet understood how dramatic Cézanne's fragility was: on the spur of the moment and for no apparent reason, he abandoned the inn at Giverny, leaving behind some unfinished canvases which Monet had to send to him; and moments of enthusiasm were inevitably followed by others of discouragement.
He lived with his mother and sister at Jas de Bouffan and then rented a cabin at the Bibémus quarry, where he spent most of his time. He often painted in the garden at the Jas, amongst the chestnut trees the leaves of which partly hid the house; in winter he could see the profile of Sainte-Victoire through the bare branches. He also painted still lifes and portraits, using local farmers as models for his canvases of card players and men smoking. When his wife and son were in Aix he had them pose for him, which was no easy task,

♦ *Paul Cézanne,* Painter with Palette, *1868-71. Pencil, 10 × 17 cm (3 15/16 × 6 5/8 in). Kunstmuseum, Basel. This drawing may be the copy of* *an illustration in Balzac's novel* The Unknown Masterpiece, *with the main character, the artist Frenhofer, touching up a canvas.*

♦ *Early 20th-century photograph of the Château Noir, with Mont Sainte-Victoire in the background. Legend has it that the château was built in the mid-19th century by a coal merchant who wanted to paint it black, hence the name. Cézanne loved to paint it from a distance, peeping* *out above the trees. "[...] I still feel keenly the vibrations of sensations created by the Provençal sun, by my childhood memories, by those horizons, those incredible profiles that leave such deep and lasting impressions." (From a letter to Henri Gasquet, 3 June 1899.)*

for Cézanne was extremely demanding. He would take a week to sketch the contours of his models, adding some shadows or indications of colour. For the still lifes he used paper flowers and artificial fruit, since he worked so slowly that real flowers and fruit would wither and rot before he could finish.
Although Cézanne had learned to apply colours more lightly, he sometimes covered his works with several layers of paint, a sign of how slowly and hard he worked. His technique varied. In some canvases the clarity of tone corresponded to the thinness of the pigment; only the dark tones consisted of many dabs of colour. In other works he used the opposite approach, with either short, broad brushstrokes or long and narrow ones, depending on the nature of the motif, the light and perhaps by his mood. Yet his technique was always dictated by, and subordinate to, sensitivity: "Technique grows in contact with nature [...] It consists in seeking to express what one feels, in organizing sensations into personal aesthetics."
His father's death in 1886 had

drastically changed his financial situation; he now had an income of 400,000 francs per year. Yet his lifestyle remained the same. He identified himself more and more with a literary character, Frenhofer, the painter who fails in the grand style in Balzac's novel *Le chef d'œuvre inconnu* (The Unknown Masterpiece). Frenhofer has been hard at work on a painting that is to be the summing up of his experience and art. One day he decides to show it to some fellow painters, but on the canvas there is nothing but a confusion of lines and colours from which emerges a magnificently painted female foot: the artist has destroyed his work with too much thought and effort. "Frenhofer, that's me," Cézanne said to Émile Bernard, who quoted a passage from Balzac's novel as the epigraph to his essay on Cézanne: "Frenhofer is passionately devoted to art, and sees farther and higher than other painters."
After his mother's death in November 1897 Paul and his sisters sold the Jas de Bouffan estate at the insistence of his brother-in-law, who was an inveterate gambler and constantly in debt. He could have kept the property by buying his sisters' shares, but perhaps he wanted to unburden himself of the weight of the memories attached to the estate, or he may have thought it did not suit his humble lifestyle.
In any case, it must have been distressing to leave the salon he had decorated as a youth, the garden with the avenue of lovely chestnut trees, the greenhouse, the low wall over which he could see Sainte-Victoire, the fields, and the farm where he had painted the day labourers playing cards. He also had to give up the seclusion that was so basic a part of his creative work, when he could observe the changing seasons, the branches with their elaborate patterns against the winter sky, the flowers in bloom in spring, the intense summer heat marked by the singing of the cicadas.
He moved to Rue Boulegon in Aix, where his housekeeper took care of him, returned to the cabin in the Bibémus quarry to paint, and rented a room in the Château Noir, halfway between Aix and Tholonet, where he often went to paint.
When Cézanne was in Paris he would go to the Louvre to draw in solitude, which was probably a substitution for painting on the motif outdoors. He copied ancient and modern sculpture, especially works by Puget, and paintings by Poussin and Rubens. He shunned the artistic milieu and even avoided his old friends if he happened

to see them in the street. His son Paul took care of his finances and even advised his father in the choice of subjects.

Despite his isolation, Cézanne's oeuvre began to attract notice. In 1888 the critic Huysmans wrote an article about him in "La Cravache," stating that he was "a revealing colourist who contributed more than the late Manet to the Impressionist movement, an artist with impaired retinas who, through his exasperated visual perception, has discovered the premonitory signs of a new art."

He was asked to participate in French and international exhibitions. In 1892 Émile Bernard published his biographical essay on Cézanne, and the following year Gustave Geffroy reproduced one of his canvases in a study of Impressionism. "Cézanne seems to be a fantastic figure," the critic Mellerio said. "Although

♦ *Cézanne's cabin near the Bibémus quarry. After the Jas de Bouffan estate was sold, the artist moved to Aix. Every day he went out to paint in seclusion in the sites where he and his childhood friends had taken walks and had gone swimming.*

living, he is spoken of as though he were dead."

His influence was beginning to make itself felt in the works of the young generation of artists. Gauguin, who called Cézanne an "Oriental mystic," said that he was striving for a definitive synthesis of art; and all the younger artists felt that he had solved the problem of maintaining the freshness of perception and its role in creation by replacing experience with

reflection. In Maurice Denis's opinion, Cézanne represented the restoration of classical tradition and the result of the great struggle for freedom that renewed modern art: he was the Poussin of Impressionism. His enigmatic works, his technique, which was at once virtuoso and simple, his totally balanced composition – and the legend of his isolated existence – had made him the central figure in the circle of avant-garde art. His almost secret production, the rare canvases in circulation, so removed from all codified rules, created a strange aura, a legendary character. Few collectors had canvases by Cézanne: Zola, Alexis, Duret, Chocquet, Dr. Gachet in Auvers, as well as Pissarro, Caillebotte, Rouart and Schuffenecker.

Père Tanguy's small shop in Rue Clauzel was the only place one could see his paintings. As Bernard recalled: "One went there as to a museum, to see the few sketches by the unknown artist who lived in Aix, dissatisfied with his work and with the world, who himself destroyed these studies, objects of admiration though they were [...] Opinions were divided, and one passed from profound discussions to bitter jeers, from insults to exaggerated praise," while Tanguy himself listened in silence. "One saw him [Tanguy] disappear into a dark room and reappear a moment later, carrying a package of modest size, carefully tied up; on his thick lips a mysterious smile, damp emotion shining in his eyes. He feverishly untied the strings and, using the back of a chair as an easel, exhibited the paintings one after the other, in religious silence." Tanguy spoke about how Cézanne was never satisfied with his work, his habit of leaving off before having finished, and his painstaking efforts, concluding: "He goes to the Louvre every morning." Many artists went to Tanguy's regularly, including Van Gogh, Denis, Signac, Seurat, Bernard and Gauguin, and they all regretted that he lived 'on the margin of life,' as Geffroy said.

'Official' recognition was yet to come. When Caillebotte died in 1894, the Luxembourg Museum had to decide whether or not to accept the collection the artist had bequeathed; in the end, only part of the collection entered the museum, including only two works by Cézanne and by Pissarro. The same year the art critic Théodore Duret sold his fine collection, including three Cézanne canvases; and upon Tanguy's death, art collector Ambroise Vollard bought his entire collection at an auction,

which prompted Geffroy to write a long article on Cézanne. Vollard then organized an exhibition of Cézanne's works, which opened in December 1895. Despite the reactionary stance of many critics, the show became the event of the year for the art collectors and younger artists.

The prices of his canvases rose, and he was asked to participate in international exhibitions. In 1901 Maurice Denis exhibited a large canvas at the Salon, *Homage to Cézanne*, representing a group of artists and friends placed around a canvas by Cézanne that had belonged to Gauguin – a sort of ideal passage, a bridge between Cézanne and the young artists – a still life that linked the heritage of Impressionism with the tradition of the Old Masters.

In the following years Cézanne took

♦ *Photograph of Gustave Geffroy. Cézanne met this art critic and writer in 1894 at Monet's residence in Giverny. Geffroy supported the Impressionist*

painters and in the mid-1890s offered to help Cézanne, whom he regarded highly. The artist began a portrait of Geffroy but left it unfinished.

♦ *Paul Cézanne, Drawing after Puget's 'Hercules,' 1884-87. Pencil, 11.8 × 19.4 cm (4 5/8 × 7 5/8 in). Private Collection. Right: Pierre Puget, Hercules, 1660-62. Marble. Musée du Louvre, Paris. Cézanne said in a letter to Charles*

Camoin (September 1903): "[...] after having seen the great masters who repose there [in the Louvre], we must hurry out and, by contact with nature, revive within ourselves the instincts, the artistic sensations that live within us."

part in important international exhibitions, as well as shows in Aix, in which he had himself listed as 'a pupil of Pissarro' in the catalogue, thus honouring the fellow artist who had guided him in his early struggles with plein-air painting and had encouraged him so much with such lofty humanity and artistic commitment.

The Motifs of the Final Years

28

A grandiose quality emanated from Cézanne in his old age, from the nasal and soothing tone of his voice, the slow, meticulous articulation of his speech. At times prolonged silence would betray unassuaged anguish; he was continuously prey to anxiety and self-doubts, the fear of not being able to reach the 'promised land.' His solitude was interrupted by meetings with young poets and writers, with whom he would go to the cafés on the Cours Mirabeau in Aix, or to the Malta Cross Hotel. But relations with him were by no means easy to maintain; the poet Joaquim Gasquet, who later wrote a book on Cézanne, saw his warm friendship with the artist turn into cold aloofness and even contempt.

The young painter Émile Bernard, who was in Aix in 1904, was welcomed by Cézanne, who invited him to work in a room near his studio; they often visited the local museum together and talked at length about art. These discussions were continued in a steady correspondence in which Cézanne, however, often betrayed impatience with Bernard's philosophical bent: "The man of letters expresses himself in abstractions, whereas the painter gives concrete shape to his sensations and perceptions by means of drawing and colour." He said that Bernard's painting procedure stemmed not from 'the emotion of nature,' but from what he had seen in museums.

Cézanne's conversations in this period are remarkable for their frequent lack of consistency. Sometimes, while working on his *Large Bathers*, he would state that painting was all in the artist's head, and would then astonish his interlocutor by insisting that art stemmed from nature and that his aim was to capture the real distance between the eye and the object, and then that it was necessary to establish harmony amongst diverse relationships which, translated in a personal register, had to be developed according to one's logical approach. He had mixed feelings about his fellow citizens of Aix; they were anything but generous towards him and yet he wanted to prove his worth to them. In fact, recognition always came from elsewhere, such as Monet who in 1895 stated that Cézanne was the greatest painter of the period, and foreign art collectors such as Karl Ernst Osthaus, founder of the Folkwang Museum, who went to visit Cézanne in Aix,

♦ *The poet and journalist Joaquim Gasquet, the son of Henri, who was a schoolfriend of Cézanne's. The Gasquets were interested in reviving a purely Provençal culture, and in various* articles Joaquim called Cézanne "the incarnation of the spirit of Provence." They became friends in 1898 and Cézanne said his relationship with Gasquet was invaluable to him.

♦ *Paul Cézanne at Les Lauves in a photograph taken by Émile Bernard in 1905. The artist wrote to Bernard that same year: "The theory to develop is that* whatever our disposition or capacity to face nature, we must reproduce what we see, forgetting everything that has been done before us."

receiving a warm welcome. On that occasion, as Osthaus later wrote, while showing him his paintings the artist remarked that the main thing in a painting was to find the distance, this is what revealed a painter's talent. "And saying this, his fingers followed the limits of the various planes on his canvas. He showed exactly how far he had succeeded in suggesting the depth and where the solution had not yet been found; here the colour had remained colour, without becoming the expression of distance." Speaking of painting in general, Cézanne called Holbein the greatest old master. "But one cannot equal Holbein," he exclaimed, "that is why I took Poussin as a model!" Among the modern artists, Cézanne spoke highly of Courbet and said that Van Gogh, Gauguin and the Neo-impressionists "make things a little too easy

for themselves." He then exclaimed: "Monet and Pissarro, the two great masters, the only ones!" He then complained of the narrow-minded provincialism that prevented him from having a female model: "An old invalid poses for all these women," he explained.

The artistic theories he expounded to his young friends were taken from Balzac's novel *The Unknown Masterpiece*, whose protagonist states that one draws – that is, isolates objects from their environment – through modelling. Like Frenhofer and all the Impressionists, for that matter, Cézanne denied the existence of the line in nature. "Pure drawing is an abstraction. Drawing and colour are not separate and distinct, since everything in nature has colour. While one paints, one draws, the more the colour harmonizes, the more precise becomes the drawing. When the colour is rich, the form is at its height." Frenhofer's theory, which

consists in starting with the protuberances that receive the most light, is reflected in an observation of Cézanne: "[...] in an orange, an apple, a ball, a head, there is a culminating point, and this point is always – in spite of the tremendous effect; light and shade, colour sensations – the closest to our eye; the edges of the objects flee towards a center on our horizon."

In order to gain a better grasp of his model, Cézanne advised Bernard to "see in nature the cylinder, the sphere, the cone, putting everything in proper perspective, so that each side of an object or a plane is directed towards a central point. Lines parallel to the horizon give breadth, that is, a section of nature [...] Lines perpendicular to this horizon give depth. But nature, for us men, is more depth than surface, hence the need to introduce

♦ *Paul Cézanne, Large Bathers, 1906. Oil on canvas, 208 × 249 cm (81 7/8 × 98 in). Philadelphia Museum of Art, W.P. Wilstach Collection. Speaking of his Bathers, Cézanne wrote to Gasquet: "It will be the painting, the one I will leave to posterity. But the center? I can't find the center [...] What should they be gathered around? Ah! Poussin's arabesque. There* was an artist who knew what he was doing. In his Baccanal at London and his Flora at the Louvre, where does the line of the bodies and landscape begin and end? It's all a unified whole. There is no center. I would like a kind of hole, a ray of light, an invisible sun to spy upon all my bodies and surround them, caress them, enhance them... precisely in the center."

in our vibrations of light – represented by reds and yellows – a sufficient quantity of blue to give the feeling of air." However, there are no cylinders, cones, no parallel or perpendicular lines. in Cézanne's works; on the contrary, as we have seen, for him the line did not exist, except as a point of contact for two planes of different colour. Thus it was that Cézanne tried to express his awareness of structure below the coloured surface presented by nature.

Cézanne's consciousness of form separated him from the Impressionists, though he never sought such an abstract concept in his oeuvre at the expense of sensation. He always found his forms in nature rather than in geometry. But his advice would have been only partial had he not shown what he meant while at work. "All things, particularly in art, are theory developed and applied in contact with nature."

He would compose still lifes by placing, with infinite care and innate taste, the objects next to one another in search of the right volumetric and chromatic balance. "The main thing is the modelling; one shouldn't even say modelling, but modulating." Bernard recalls: "He started with the shadow and with a brushstroke, then covered it with another, larger one, then a third, until all the spots of tones, forming a kind of screen, modelled the object in colour." The old artist advised Bernard to "begin lightly and with almost neutral tones. Then one must proceed by steadily climbing the scale and tightening the chromatics." Cézanne had told the critic Geffroy that he wanted to astonish Paris with

♦ *The pine tree in front of the caves near the Château Noir. Ardengo Soffici wrote in 1929: "Like Michelangelo, Cézanne understood the mystical power that bursts from silent things, from tree trunks and rocks [...] his oeuvre is a rough, bare, rocky, atrocious,* *lacerated terrain in which plants, flowers and grass bloom sadly, chastely, with simple, natural spontaneity. [...] Without a law, without scruples, his style bears the ruggedness of the outlines of his beings and what surrounds them."*

an apple, and in fact he carefully studied the forms and colours of this fruit, which he considered the motif *par excellence*. The breadth and solidity of some of his compositions in which broad drapery is combined with fruit composed in a complex but well-balanced manner, justify the principle whereby the apple for Cézanne was as important as the human body.

As he grew older, Cézanne confined himself more and more to Aix and the surrounding territory. Though he had more than enough money to travel, he did nothing to change his simple, austere lifestyle; he was more than content to work and remain in a world that was so familiar to him. While on a sojourn with his family at Lake Annecy in 1896, he wrote to his friend Solari: "The lake is very nice with the big mountains all round [...] But when one was born down there, it is no use, nothing else seems to mean anything." In order to find solitary places where he could paint without being disturbed, he hired a carriage. When he could not stop where he had found a good motif because it was private property, he would get down and walk so as not to tire the horse. "The world does not understand me," he told the coachman, "and I do not understand the world." He avoided L'Estaque, once so picturesque and now spoiled by too many people and too much 'progress.'

Only the True Is Beautiful

After Jas de Bouffan was sold, Cézanne had difficulty in finding a place to work in. He began painting at the Bibémus quarry, near Tholonet, from where he could go to the Château Noir and its woods, which had a view of Sainte-Victoire. He sometimes painted in the garden of the house in Rue Boulegon in Aix, but it was not large and quiet enough for him. So he went into the country, taking the old road to Sainte-Victoire

♦ *Mont Sainte-Victoire seen from the hills of Les Lauves. Cézanne discovered a new viewpoint of the mountain from here: the unmistakeable shape was still quite* *large despite the distance. The truncated cone seen from the Bibémus quarry road is now a rugged, irregular triangle which, after a sharp drop, descends gently to the Cengle hills.*

♦ *Early 20th-century photograph of Cézanne's studio at Les Lauves. In November 1901 he* *bought a plot of land on the hills north of Aix, and had the house built the following year.*

which, after a series of curves and rises and falls, opens out onto a undulating plain that stretches to the foot of the mountain. From a vantage point two pines can be seen, with the mountain in the background. The path leads to the Maison Maria and then, with meadows here and there, to the Château Noir, the bizarre late 19th-century construction consisting of two buildings with narrow neo-gothic windows and steep roofs connected by a series of pillars originally planned as an orangery that give it the appearance of a ruin. According to legend, it was built by a coal merchant

or an alchemist, hence the name; but it was actually built of lovely yellow stone from the Bibémus quarry, the same used in the mansions and churches of Aix. The path then proceeds to a level space filled with blocks of stone lying here and there, free-growing vegetation. tree trunks and a huge abandoned millstone and ancient cistern. Cézanne loved this spot and often painted here.

In Cézanne's canvases the Château Noir is always seen from a distance among the tree tops, because he preferred to work in the woods, climb up the hill, where the sky was hidden amongst the branches, and then reach the top with a group of rocks that formed caves hidden amidst the vegetation. This was a remote, intimate spot of wild, secluded beauty, the kind of site Cézanne loved because he could identify himself with it. He rounded off the boulders, giving them a softer form, connecting their curves in a sensual rhythm.

He faithfully depicted their irregular shapes, the crevices and nooks that cast shadows.

Provence has a vast number of old quarries, some of which have been abandoned for centuries and centuries. The stones with their complex, bizarre shapes lie under a cloudless sky. The stone at the Bibémus quarry, beaten by the mistral, is especially interesting, as it seems to

have soaked up the rays of the sun; it was excavated manually, without superstructures, which created fascinating, mysterious conformations: an immense complex of huge holes, often in the shape of steps. Nearby is Les Infernets gorge, where Zola's father had designed the dam that provides Aix with water; after forty years, Cézanne returned to one of the favourite sites of his childhood. Trees and bushes had emerged amidst the rocks; the area was exposed to the sun and wind, and the solitary boulders created a wild architecture that seemed

30

to have been built by prehistoric giants.

It was here that Cézanne embarked on a series of paintings, executed from 1895 to 1899, that attempt to assemble this chaotic configuration of stones into a coherent unity of pictorial planes set on the surface of the canvas. The rock formations obstruct the onlooker's view, and the fantastic character of the site is underscored by the orange hues of the rock which makes such a contrast with the green vegetation and the blue sky. This unreal atmosphere betrays the artist's state of mind.

The need for a change led Cézanne to look for a studio where he could work on the large compositions of bathers he had in mind. In 1901 he bought a small property on the hill of Les Lauves, which overlooks Aix. The second floor of the small house he built there was a large studio about four meters high, the northern wall of which was a huge window; near this is a long slit that he used to insert the large canvases. On the opposite wall there were two large windows with a view of Aix and, in the distance, the Chaîne de l'Etoile mountains. An old gardener – Vallier – took care of the grounds. Cézanne would climb up the hill, as there was a lovely panorama at the top. Here Sainte-Victoire was no longer the truncated cone that one saw from the Château Noir and the Bibémus quarry, but an irregular triangle dominating a vast plain: a jumble of horizontal and vertical lines, a thick network of colours, a view so wide it was hard to take in. In the southern light, the mountain, the symbol of Provence, obsessed Cézanne, becoming the exclusive motif of his final landscapes.

In these works the mountain was part of the surrounding countryside; a rich and thick texture of colours envelops a clear shape that blends in with nature, lending warmth and density to the image. Much like an epic sculpture, the mountain is created by means of a series of tonal contrasts that transform the motif into a variegated fabric of corresponding values, in a free play of forms and colours. Here the true innovative aspect of Cézanne triumphs – the modulation of colour. "At times I conceive colours as vast, noumenal entities, ideas with a physical presence, creatures of pure reason, with whom we can enter into relations. Nature is not an affair of the surface; it is in depth. Colours express that depth on the surface. They arise from the roots of the world. They are its life, the life of ideas." In Sainte-Victoire, which is pure form, a pretext to delve more deeply into his pictorial

research, Cézanne found a new field of perception. The plain in the foreground is rendered through the juxtaposition of patches of colour; he does away with all notions of depth, and the mountain is right upon the viewer. Its image is absorbed in a series of facets that, far from being the negation of reality, are a procedure whereby each particle of earth is reproduced with the rigour of a geologist. "To paint a landscape properly," Cézanne told Gasquet, "I first have to know the geological strata [...] One fine morning, next day, the geological fundaments are gradually revealed to me, the layers of strata, the great plan of my canvas, and in my mind's eye I trace the skeleton of stone [...] I start to acquire some detachment from the landscape, to see it. This first sketch, these geological lines – they are what releases me from it. Geometry, the yardstick of the Earth."
After this phase, Cézanne worked on the modulation of colour, the structure of which was based on the

♦ *View of Aix-en-Provence from Cézanne's studio at Les Lauves. From the large terrace the view of the town is magnificent, with the Pilon du Roi standing out in the Etoile range. The property also had a little garden, which the old gardener Vallier took care of. Cézanne confided to Gasquet: "Where is Aix, the old Aix of Zola and Baille, the dear streets of the old quarter, the grass shooting up from the pavement, the oil lamps [...] Yes, oil lighting, and not that crude electricity that violates the mystery of the city, while our old lights tinged them with golden hues and made them fiery, permeated them as in Rembrandt."*

♦ *Maurice Denis, Paying a Visit to Cézanne, 1906. J.-F. Denis Collection, Alençon. In this canvas, besides Cézanne holding the palette, there is Denis seated at right and K.X. Roussel at left. A great admirer of Cézanne, Denis was a painter and writer.*

construction of nature. Through colour his concept was transformed into an image that was at once solid and fluid, achieving a balance between a constantly changing creation and its immutable, geologically determined framework.

In his studio at Les Lauves, Cézanne kept objects that he used for his still lifes: jars, bottles, skulls, crockery and a sort of table cover that served as a backdrop. Together with these beloved objects he furnished the studio with a wooden table, a plaster putto attributed to the sculptor Puget, and a statuette of a flayed man; on the walls he hung various photographs or lithographs of works by old masters such as Signorelli and Rubens as well as by Delacroix, and in a corner was a ladder that he used to paint his *Large Bathers* canvases. His male bathers, who are related to his childhood when together with Zola he bathed on the banks of the rivers in Provence, are always in less compact groups, while the composition of his female nudes, inspired by the poses of the models he copied at the Louvre, was structured much more rigorously. The erotic themes of his youthful fantasy are now transposed into less unsettling subjects, while still retaining traces of the former tension and conflict, which can be seen in the unusual, even ambiguous, atmosphere. The figures with their elemental poses and almost primitive nature are harbingers of modern art while at the same time being closely related to the great examples of the past. The *Bathers* canvases, highly original works that had such a marked influence on 20th-century art, are often linked to Cézanne's curious statement that he wanted "to redo Poussin after nature." But his relationship with classical art must not be mistaken for slavishness; the Old Masters, including Poussin, were a source of knowledge and inspiration for Cézanne, and only that. Artistic intellect that was not accompanied by a study of nature was sterility: "The Louvre is good for reference, but it must be only a go-between; the true and wonderful study to be undertaken is that of the infinite variety of nature."

*A*ttaining the Absolute

Cézanne's dream of retrieving the lost unity between man and nature is reflected in these works. The *Bathers* were both a meditation on the past and nostalgia for the harmonious existence of myths, albeit still deeply rooted in the artist's emotional conflicts. The figures were gradually stripped of any personal reference and became detached, almost neutral, thus indicating an idyllic state of freedom and harmony.

Though he lived in Aix, he would go to the studio at Les Lauves quite early in the morning, usually returning to town around eleven. But he would sometimes stay there to work through the day. Around four o'clock in the afternoon, he took a carriage to paint outdoors, waiting until the shadows lengthened on the landscape and the

♦ Cézanne photographed by K.X. Roussel while painting at Les Lauves in 1906. He wrote the following to Émile Bernard on 21 September 1906: "I continue to study nature, drawing after her, and I seem to be making some progress, albeit slowly. I am old and ill, and I have sworn to die painting rather than to waste away vilely in the manner that threatens old men who allow themselves to be dominated by passions that coarsen their senses. I believe in the logical realization of what we see and feel before nature. [...] Hearty greetings from an immensely stubborn old man."

air became crystal-clear, when objects in the distance were especially sharp and the foreground glistened in the rays of the receding sun. When it was particularly hot, Cézanne worked on the terrace, doing watercolours of the town in the distance or canvases of the old gardener Vallier or other

peasants. The portraits of Vallier reveal how Cézanne had attained inner peace, a true harmony that makes his art the expression of timelessness and the eternal. In his final years, having abandoned motifs such as the Château Noir and the Bibémus quarry, Cézanne painted the motifs near his studio or worked on the bathers or on still lifes. Already in 1892 Félix Fénéon had said that "three apples of Cézanne strike and move one, they are even mystical." These canvases belong to the domain of pure painting. His relationship with so-called inanimate objects was fundamental for him; the correspondences, relations and tension among things were anything but mere formal play, for him they conveyed the basic flux of life. "Objects influence one another totally [...] They spread their influence imperceptibly about, by means of their

♦ Cézanne in front of his 1906 version of the Large Bathers, in a photograph by Émile Bernard. With his idea of 'redoing Poussin after nature' he tackled one of the great motifs of his final years. The original play of volumes and the theme itself of the bathers, rendered through a violent break with traditional canons, was to prove to be a decisive influence, in the early 20th century, on Matisse, Derain, Picasso and Braque.

auras, as we do by means of looks and words. Chardin was the first to sense this, he captured the atmosphere of objects in gradations of colour [...] There was nothing he ignored. He got that contact of the minute particles that are around things, the life-particles that surround things." The German poet Rilke gave a striking description of how Cézanne weighed the pictorial elements, stating that the "two processes of appropriation and putting what was appropriated to a personal use were opposed in him [...] constantly at variance." Although they are related, they betrayed his own inner conflicts; forms and colours, acting together to lend balance and harmony to the whole, also nurtured its secret tensions. Linking his motifs was for Cézanne the first stage of perception, which was followed by the definition of pictorial space. He made use of multiple perspective or vantage points; the objects were connected – and at the same time had their own space – through the interaction of linear construction, colour modulation, and brushwork. Every element thus became part of a greater conflict between depth and surface. The apple for him represented the mythical dream of erotic realization as well as the expression of the variety

of human relationships. "I decided against flowers," he told Gasquet, "they wither on the instant. Fruits are more loyal, as if they were asking forgiveness for having lost their colour. The idea exudes from them together with their fragrance. They appear with all their scents, they speak of the fields they have left behind, the rain that nourished them, the dawns they have seen. When you render the skin of a lovely peach in rich, bold strokes, or the melancholy of an old apple, you sense their mutual reflections, the same gentle shadow of relinquishment, the same loving sun, the same memory of dew." Starting off from the visible, Cézanne was totally dedicated to the patient perception of things, which was always connected to finding different levels of symbolic meanings for them. This can be seen above all in his merging of different planes, the

mutual heightening of colours, the harmonious interaction of the various elements, all of which have a common base – the fullness and richness of life. "There are two thousand politicians in every legislature, but there is a Cézanne only every two centuries!" the artist once asserted, well aware of his talent and yet always tormented by doubts. His religious conversion, his "participation in the Middle Age," as he called it, was not so much due to a fear of death as to a fear of not being able to attain his artistic objectives. Illness and old age aggravated his eccentric traits. In late May 1906 he attended the unveiling of an unfinished bust of Zola by Solari that had been donated to the Aix library. The tribute to his old friend brought back memories and Cézanne burst into tears.

In the last summer of his life he took a carriage to the banks of the Arc River, not far from the Jas de Bouffan, where he found shade and seclusion. "I do not have the magnificent richness of colouring that animates nature. Here on the banks of the river there are so many subjects, and the same one seen from a different angle makes a powerful and interesting study, so varied that I think I could be busy for months without moving from the spot and merely leaning sometimes more to the right, sometimes more to the left." He expressed his desire to die painting to Bernard, and his wish was fulfilled. A violent storm caught him by surprise on 15 October 1906 while he was working on a landscape a few hundred meters from his studio. He lay unconscious, exposed to the rain for hours, and was finally picked up and taken to Aix. The next day he got out of bed and went to work on a portrait

of Vallier in the garden, but soon collapsed. He died on October 23, 1906 without seeing his son and wife again. A few weeks later, they removed all his paintings from the Lauves studio and sold many of them right off. Others were later bought by Vollard and Bernheim-Jeune, providing Cézanne's family with a large sum of money (added to the inheritance of Cézanne's father's fortunes). But since Hortense was an inveterate gambler and their son seemed to have a talent for losing money, they squandered the entire fortune. The writer Marcel Provence bought the Lauves studio in 1921. When he died in 1954, a committee headed by James Lord and John Rewald raised the money needed to buy the studio, which they donated to the University of Aix-en-Provence.

31

THE WORKS

"*M. Cézanne is, in his works, a Greek
of the golden age; his canvases have the calm
and heroic serenity of the paintings
and terracottas of antiquity and the ignorant
who laugh at the* Bathers, *for example,
impress me like the Barbarians criticizing
the Parthenon.*"

Georges Rivière, "L'Impressionniste," 14 April 1877

Biography

Cézanne's life was dominated by solitude, consecrated to painting, and presented no sensational events to speak of. His existence was governed by his artistic vocation, just as his painting (especially in his later years) concentrated on a few, select motifs – still lifes, bathers, the Provence landscape – which he continuously elaborated and refined in a process of vertical penetration, as it were, with the aim of conquering a dimension of the absolute.

His links with his native land were also part of this exclusivist stance – though his relations with Paris were indispensable to his career and he underwent the influence of the Île-de-France landscape which, during his so-called Impressionist period, was a basic factor in his artistic development and sensitivity. In fact, this was to remain a subtle influence throughout his lifetime; he would periodically return to Pontoise to paint with Pissarro, and in 1892 he bought a house at Marlotte in the Fontainebleau forest, the classical site of the Barbizon school painters and the Impressionists.

But Cézanne's roots lay in Provence. The countryside around Aix-en-Provence – the town in which he was born on 19 January 1839 – where as an adolescent he roved with his buddies Zola and Baille, was his prime source of inspiration.

His family, which he did not love when he was young because he felt they did not understand and appreciate him, became in his mature years an emotional refuge for him, especially his mother and his sister Marie.
The latter even succeeded in having him turn to religion; the atheist became a practising Catholic in the 1890s.

His relationship with Hortense Fiquet, with whom he lived from 1869 and whom he married in 1886, was a total failure, a disappointment and frustrating bond almost from the outset. Nor was his rapport with his son Paul without blemishes. Despite Cézanne's infatuation for his son in his

later years, young Paul (who was born on 4 January 1872) suffered from the lack of a united family as well as from his father's rather indifferent attitude when he was small.

Cézanne was also born out of wedlock: his parents, Louis-Auguste, a hat dealer and exporter, and Anne-Élisabeth-Honorine Aubert, were not married, not even when Paul's sister Marie was born on 4 July 1841. Their marriage finally took place on 29 January 1844, and only their third child, Rose, was born into a legally recognized family on 30 June 1854. Louis-Auguste's fine business sense guaranteed a good living for the family. His originally uninfluential social status grew somewhat in 1847 when he bought a bank in financial straits in 1847, founding with a partner the Cézanne & Cabassol Bank, which would be the only one in town for a long time. In 1859 Cézanne *père* bought the Jas de Bouffan, a fine estate outside of town, but the rigid high society in Aix continued to consider him a parvenu; despite the fortune he had amassed, his original social status and inferior cultural background were not forgotten, or forgiven.

Paul had a good education: from 1844 to 1849 he attended the elementary school in Rue des Epinaux, from 1848 to 1852 went to the École Saint-Joseph, and from 1852 to 1858 was a boarder at the Collège Bourbon, where the cream of the Aix bourgeoisie received its education. Here he acquired a solid humanistic culture and met Émile Zola, one of the cornerstones of his artistic and sentimental life. Zola was the friend of his adolescence, with whom he shared sentiments and creative urges, cultural and existential experiences and dreams; but later on his friend would prove to be a great disappointment for Cézanne. His relationship with the future novelist is represented cryptically in many of his early canvases and, in the latter part of his life, is evoked in an indirect but compelling manner in the landscapes

that depict the sites of their childhood *camaraderie*.
Cézanne's friendship with Zola was marked by intensity, passion, emulation, trust, and abandon. It was Zola who helped him to discover his true vocation and who insisted that Paul join him in Paris, where he had gone in 1858, and where Cézanne finally went for a brief stay in 1861 and settled in 1862. He was prey to doubts, and wavered between obedience to his father's wishes that he become a lawyer or a member of his bank administration, and his ardent desire to follow his artistic calling. He enrolled in the faculty of law at the University of Aix in 1859, but in 1861 abandoned his studies and set off for Paris to become a painter.

His relations with the French capital were to be a thorn in his side for the rest of his life. He always felt uncomfortable in Paris; it was alien to his nature. He was provincial and, indeed, chose to remain so, hiding his shyness, pride and sensitivity behind coarse manners and mocking irony that he had inherited from his father. Paris was the main scene of Cézanne's many artistic 'fiascos,' which hurt him deeply but, instead of crushing him, triggered a rebellious, defiant reaction. In 1862 he failed to pass the entrance examination at the École des Beaux-Arts; the following year, though he exhibited at the Salon des Refusés, he was not even mentioned in the catalogue; from 1862 to 1882 he was rejected by the Salon jury and his canvases were the object of insults and derision. He exposed himself to disfavour in 1866 by asking the Count de Nieuwerkerke, the Director of Fine Arts, to revive the Salon des Refusés, and urged Zola to take a stand. His friend complied by writing articles in "L'Événement" that laid bare the favouritism and irregular practices of the Salon jury.

Cézanne's fiery independence and lack of interest in anything not connected with his artistic labour were reflected in his behaviour at the outbreak of the Franco-Prussian War in 1870. He did

not answer the call-up and went to live in L'Estaque, a fishermen's village near Marseilles, with Hortense Fiquet, the model he had been living with for a year. When the Third Republic was proclaimed in 1870 he was elected member of the commission for the Free Municipal School for Drawing in Aix, where he had first studied art from 1857 on, but he never participated in the Commission proceedings. Totally extraneous to the events of the Paris Commune, he returned to the capital in September 1871, when order had been re-established.

His working companionship with Pissarro, which dated from 1863, when they met at the Académie Suisse, reached its height when Cézanne stayed in Pontoise and Auvers-sur-Oise from 1872 to 1874. Pissarro's unique personality nurtured a relationship that ended only when the older artist died on 19 November 1903. Cézanne followed Pissarro's advice to a great extent, even copying one of the latter's views of Louveciennes; he regularly went with him to paint 'on the motif' and was most grateful for Pissarro's demonstration of human and artistic generosity and rectitude.

This was Cézanne's so-called Impressionist period, when he struck up a friendship with Dr. Gachet, who had built a lovely house in Auvers and taught him the secrets of engraving, and when he was also close to Monet, Renoir and the other Impressionist artists. Cézanne cemented this relationship by participating in the first exhibition of the group which took place in Nadar's studio in the Boulevard des Capucines from 15 April to 15 May 1874. Although Count Doria purchased his *The House of the Hanged Man*, he was the target of particularly violent attacks on the part of the critics, especially for *A Modern Olympia*, which seemed to aggravate the scandal aroused by Manet's canvas of the same name at the Salon des Refusés in 1863.
The following years were marked by a

certain lack of understanding between Cézanne and Zola, who was rapidly becoming a successful novelist. In 1865 he had published *La confession de Claude*, which he had dedicated to Cézanne and Baille; in 1873 he came out with *Le ventre de Paris*, in which he created the character of the painter Claude Lantier, modelled after Cézanne. Now famous, Zola tended to separate his public image from that of his artist friends, who were having an extremely difficult time in gaining recognition. Zola felt he was the only one who had faithfully interpreted the aesthetics of naturalism and viewed their painting more as a commendable endeavour than a real achievement. In particular he detached himself from Cézanne, as he was increasingly convinced that his friend was an 'abortive genius.' Their different social aspirations and lifestyles did the rest, though the definitive break in their relations came about only in 1886 with the publication of Zola's novel *L'Œuvre*. The suicide of the main character, the painter Claude Lantier, seemed to Cézanne to be an irrevocable judgement of his inevitable failure as an artist; it was not only the tragic epilogue of a fictional story, but also marked the end of a real-life experience. From the mid-1870s Cézanne began to acquire a limited number of admirers, including Victor Chocquet, whom he had met in 1875. One of the artist's portraits of his new friend caused an uproar in the third Impressionist exhibition of 1877, which included seventeen works by Cézanne. Philip Leroy, the critic for "Charivari" – the same person who, upon seeing Monet's *Impression, Sunrise* at the 1874 Impressionist exhibition, had mockingly coined the term 'Impressionism' – wrote that it was not advisable for a pregnant woman to linger in front of that canvas, as it might cause the child to catch yellow fever before it was even born. But Georges Rivière, in *L'Impressionniste*, which was published for the occasion, praised

Cézanne, calling him the artist who was "the most attacked, the most mistreated by the press and the public for the past fifteen years."
Cézanne's financial status was by no means brilliant, and Zola had to come to his aid from time to time. The break between the two was still a thing of the future; during Cézanne's sojourns at the author's château at Médan from 1878 to 1885 there was no sign of the end of their friendship. On the other hand, his relations with his father were tense, and he did not have the courage to tell him of his liaison with Hortense; however, his father suspected something of the kind, kept a tight hold on his purse strings and complained about Paul's lack of interest in his family.
In 1882 Cézanne finally gained admission to the Salon, not because the jury had selected him, but thanks to a rule whereby each jury member was allowed to present one of his students, which his friend Guillemet did. After this experience, the Salon jury continued to reject him. Though he still went to paint at Pontoise with Pissarro, he saw less and less of his other fellow artists, and had not taken part in their exhibitions since 1877. Impressionism was in a critical stage and each artist was taking his own path in search of a solution. They all met once again at Manet's funeral on 3 May 1883, and on Monet's fifty-fourth birthday (14 November 1891) Cézanne went to Giverny, where he met Clemenceau, Rodin, Geffroy and Mary Cassatt.
His visits to Paris were few and far between. He took refuge in L'Estaque, Gardanne, and the Jas de Bouffan estate. But despite his seclusion, his works began to become known in Paris. In 1883 Père Tanguy sold one of his canvases to Gauguin and another one to Signac the following year.
In 1885 a mysterious love affair with an unknown woman rekindled his passion, but it was short-lived.
The following year, in fact, he finally married Hortense in both a civil and religious ceremony, which took place

in Aix on April 28 and 29 in the presence of his family. The same year his father died at 88, leaving the family a fortune.
By this time Cézanne had taken up permanent residence in Provence. But his fame was spreading. In 1888 Huysmans wrote an article about him, in 1889 *The House of the Hanged Man* was shown at the Universal Exposition, and in 1890 three of his canvases were exhibited at the "Les XX" show in Brussels. In 1892 Émile Bernard published his first essay on Cézanne (the second came out in 1904). At the auction sale of Père Tanguy's collection in 1894 – the paint dealer had died the preceding year – Ambroise Vollard, who had opened a gallery in Rue Lafitte, bought six of Cézanne's works; the following year he organized a one-man show, for which Cézanne sent him 150 canvases. In 1897 Vollard bought all the canvases in the artist's studio from his son Paul.
Cézanne systematically went through the countryside of Aix in search of motifs. He rented a cabin at the Bibémus quarry and often painted there, and also tried to buy the Château Noir, another fascinating site filled with childhood memories. In 1897 two of his canvases were placed in the Luxembourg Museum together with the other paintings by the Impressionists left by the Caillebotte bequest. The artist had donated his collection to the French state, on condition that it be accepted in its entirety; but the state did not comply with Caillebotte's wishes and accepted only part of the donation.
The death of his mother on 25 October 1897 and of his childhood friend, the painter Achille Emperaire, in 1898 left a void in his existence. The sale of the Jas de Bouffan estate the following year marked a definitive break with his past. He went to live in Aix and intensified his search for interesting motifs in the countryside.
In 1899, 1900 and 1902 Cézanne's works were exhibited at the Salon des Indépendants in Paris. The art

collector Chocquet died in April 1895 and Isaac de Camondo bought *The House of the Hanged Man* at the auction sale for 6,200 francs, while international art collector Durand-Ruel began to buy Cézanne's canvases.
In 1900 the artist went to the Centennial Exhibition in Paris, where three of his works were being shown. The following year Maurice Denis exhibited his *Homage to Cézanne*, which was later purchased by the author André Gide. That same year Cézanne's works were on exhibit in Brussels, where he returned in 1904. In 1901 Cézanne had bought a property at Les Lauves, where he had a studio built the following year. More and more of his canvases were being exhibited, and friends and admirers went to visit him: Vollard, Bernheim-Jeune, Bernard, and the German art collector Osthaus. Having himself listed as a 'pupil of Pissarro,' he also exhibited his works at the Société des Amis des Arts in Aix in 1902, overcoming his aversion to his fellow citizens.
In March 1903, ten of Cézanne's canvases were sold at the auction sale of Zola's collection (Cézanne's friend had died on 29 September 1902); the artist also exhibited his works in Vienna, Berlin and Paris. The Cassirer Gallery in Berlin organized his second one-man show, and in October the Impressionist exhibition at the Richter Gallery in Dresden also included works by Cézanne. In 1905 Vollard had an exhibit of the artist's watercolours, and Durand-Ruel included ten of his canvases in the large Impressionist show at the Grafton Galleries in London.
Cézanne continued to paint outdoors. In July 1906 he worked near the Cabanon de Jourdan, in August he was on the banks of the Arc river despite a case of bronchitis, and in October he withstood the mistral in order to do watercolours in the Beauregard sector. He died in his home in Aix on 23 October 1906 after being caught in a violent storm while he was painting in the countryside.

Cézanne's Early Works

The youthful production of Cézanne is marked by an enigmatic beauty, a rough-hewn grandeur. The motifs are connected to his moods and obsessions, which were translated into powerful, crude forms, brusque movements, dense pictorial compositions. His portraits, scenes inspired by his imagination, still lifes and landscapes are shot through with a violence that betrays the brutality that according to him informed artistic creation.

The 1861 and 1863 sojourns in Paris introduced Cézanne to the old masters as well as to the young avant-garde artists who gathered around Manet. The example of the great artists of the past, from the Venetians to Caravaggio to Ribera, accompanied his admiration for Delacroix and for Courbet's realism. Small erotic canvases in the Venetian style reveal an unbridled fantasy that was not without a certain coarseness; an overriding attraction for large subjects found expression in copies, the most interesting of which is that of Delacroix's *Dante and Vergil in Hell* (1864). The panels of the *Four Seasons* in the alcove of the Jas de Bouffan salon (1860-62) confirm Cézanne's indebtedness to tradition: the Quattrocento artists and Tintoretto. His most important canvas in this period is *Portrait of Louis-Auguste Cézanne* (1862), a massive and cadenced interpretation of contemporary realism. His friendship with Pissarro, who made his debut in the Salon in 1864 as a pupil of Corot, and his meeting with the other young painters at the Académie Suisse – including Monet, Bazille and Renoir – injected new influences into his art. In the mid-1860s his still lifes reflected the technique of artists working in the Courbet manner as well as in the Spanish tradition, such as Ribot and Bonvin; the presence of Chardin, with his repertory of common objects pervaded by the marks of truth, was strongly felt; and Manet was a fundamental influence in the handling of impastoed, flatly coloured areas (*Still Life with Bread and Eggs*, 1865). His landscapes of the same period, with their large, dark, summarily worked masses, are close to Corot and the Barbizon school. Leaves and rocks intertwine, heralding a trait that would become characteristic in his later oeuvre: the construction of form through brushstrokes or through the juxtaposition of areas of colour rendered with a palette knife. Cézanne's portraits, even the small ones, took on a monumental character and his procedure astonished his friends. Lawyers in their robes, monks in tunics, craftsmen wearing smocks and berets and common people stare at us intensely; his uncle Dominique Aubert posed for about a dozen canvases, which Cézanne executed quite rapidly. Having adopted Courbet's spatula, he now applied it to Manet's flat colours and tonal contrasts, creating a singular, forceful style.

The most interesting portrait in this phase is *Portrait of the Artist's Father Reading "L'Événement"* (1866), a work perfectly in tune with Zola's conception of art as the revelation of the artist himself who is able to achieve perfection through his creative skill. Instead of the conservative newspaper his father usually read, Cézanne portrayed him holding the paper that published Zola's revolutionary art criticism in 1866. On the wall is a still life the young artist had executed with a palette knife. The canvases executed in this style are an exceptional and unique body of works in Cézanne's oeuvre. Thirty years later, when he saw some of them propped against a wall in his studio, he indicated their sensual character by calling them "*couillard* painting"; with this crude reference to virility, the artist points out how these works symbolize the brutal assault on the material properties of painting as well as the very essence of his temperament. When he left the Jas de Bouffan in 1897 his conception of art had greatly changed, and he destroyed many of the large canvases of this period. But they are important works which – as Lawrence Gowing says – engender form in the modern sense of the word, building the structure of the picture through painterly technique. While doing this, he accentuated the most 'subversive' aspect of Courbet's art, realistic tangibility, by means of bold and obsessive thick textures. Whereas Monet, Renoir and Pissarro attenuated Courbet's procedure and Manet ignored structural tonal correspondences, Cézanne created an important precursory style. The only fellow artist who understood this was Pissarro, who in 1867 executed a still life in the Cézanne style, drawing inspiration from works in which the form was modelled with the solidity of sculpture. In his landscapes Cézanne also created impasto colour zones.

Though he had decided to paint with great vigour, highlighting the dissonances between style and subject, Cézanne himself was surprised by the results he had achieved, in which the power of execution was rendered by the liberating violence of the colours. Soon new experimental elements came into play. In *The Negro Scipio* (1867), a black model at the Académie Suisse, he resorts to a more linear manner of applying the paint and a rhythmic movement that would be utilized up to 1870 in works of fantastic and heightened tension. The most singular work of this period is *The Rape* (or *The Abduction*), a violent scene painted for Zola in the romantic, erotic, almost morbid climate of the author's contemporaneous works. The composition, with the two bodies standing out against the backdrop of Sainte-Victoire, seems to be indebted to a tradition that goes from Tintoretto to Puget and Daumier, and the controlled refulgence of the colour opens new perspectives for the artist. The same turbulent atmosphere is to be found in Cézanne's masterpiece with a religious subject, which was later cut in half. *Christ in Limbo* and *Mary Magdalene* (or *Sorrow*, 1867), which was perhaps connected to a traditional Easter motif and was executed as a decoration for the Jas de Bouffan salon. Despite the lack of proportion between the two halves, the harmony of the whole is maintained and Cézanne's borrowings from the past (especially from Sebastiano del Piombo) are enhanced by his bold handling of the subject. The artist's indebtedness to the old masters can also be seen in *The Autopsy* (or *Preparation for a Funeral*, 1869) and *The Murder* (1867-70): the same bald head of Caravaggesque derivation, the same violence in which expression and intensity overwhelm drawing. Furthermore, both these works bear the influence of popular newspaper accounts and Zola's novels, especially *Thérèse Raquin*.

Towards the end of the 1860s Cézanne's production becomes more prolific and he addresses a wider range of motifs; a series of imaginary landscapes, albeit based on various sites in the Aix and L'Estaque countryside, present industrial scenes, somewhat similar to what Pissarro was doing and, in the field of literature, to Zola. This series is characterized by a thick impasto (which, however, was lighter than that in his preceding canvases), summary handling, and contrasting colours (*Factories in front of the Mont du Cengle*, 1869-70). Soon afterwards there is a heightening of tumultuous movement and a new sensation of imbalance: *Melting Snow at L'Estaque* (1870) seems to be a vision of a world in disintegration that slides down the steep diagonal of the hill. Outdoor scenes alternate with disturbing indoor ones: in the 1869-70 version of *Paul Alexis Reading to Zola* (1869-70), two large self-absorbed figures with lowered eyes stand out in an empty space; *Overture to Tannhäuser* (1869-70) is a scene of sublimated domestic life. Another subject taken from family life and translated into a timeless domain is *Portrait of Achille Emperaire* (c. 1868). The large lettering on the top of the canvas serves to emphasize the spatial structure of the work, as in Tintoretto or Velázquez; this portrayal of his artist friend – whose head is almost twice the normal size and who has a pathetic, mournful look and disproportionate body – takes on a formal, hieratic character. The areas of shadow, which surround the figure or are projected onto it, are veined with tenderness.

As for the artist's landscapes, the quest for order and stability that would characterize his later works, began to make itself felt around 1870. In *The Railway Cutting* (1869-70), the oblique ascending lines seek an equilibrium that corresponds to structures set on the surface of the canvas with rigorous symmetry. The corners of this composition seem to be connected by an echo pattern that highlights the visual components rather than the subject through a new pictorial procedure of developing parallel elements. The deep gash in the earth is balanced by Sainte-Victoire rising up to the sky over a horizon that suggests the blue hues of the sea. Cézanne's 1870 landscapes of L'Estaque are quite original, but an even more mysterious aspect of his oeuvre are the subject pictures that may have been executed at Aix a few months earlier.

In *Pastoral* (or *Idyll*, c. 1870) Cézanne depicts himself in the guise of a dreamer reclining amidst female nudes; his pose reminds one of the melancholy Byronian protagonist in Delacroix's *The Death of Sardanapalus*. He has crossed the lake in a windless night, on a boat whose sails are still hoisted. The violent hues herald an ominous event and the surroundings are filled with phallic symbols. The genre painting tradition, from Giorgione to Watteau to Manet, is here transformed into an excruciating scene. Cézanne's method of making the landscape dynamic through vaguely human forms is quite unusual for the painting of the time; he over-interprets, as it were, the natural elements in the composition, allusively projecting into them the feelings of the characters.

In *The Temptation of St. Anthony* the figure of Cézanne is thinly veiled in the garb of the saint, and the work is permeated with that "long-suffering, subterranean and distressed character" that Baudelaire saw in Flaubert's work of the same name. A trio of female nudes occupies the foreground; the one at the far right with the gloomy air and masculine features is remarkably similar to the portrait of the young Zola that Cézanne had worked on from 1862 to 1864. In the solitude of his radical pictorial procedure, the artist reinvented visual sensations and emotions, introducing a tempestuous atmosphere and conveying the sense of an imperious inner illumination to the scene.

In his search for a style suitable for the representation of a mythical banquet, Cézanne in *The Feast* (or *The Orgy*) drew inspiration from the most famous scene in Second Empire painting, Couture's *Romans of the Decadence* and its prototype, Veronese's *Marriage at Cana*, a masterpiece that was a favourite amongst the exponents of *peinture claire*. But compared to these historical antecedents, Cézanne's canvas seems to get out of control; the figures and objects spill over one another, as if driven by a whirlwind, overwhelmed by unrestrained emotions. Besides Nebuchadnezzar's banquet in Flaubert's *Temptation of St. Anthony*, the literary sources of this painting include Flaubert's *Salammbô* and Dido's feast in the first book of Vergil's *Aeneid*.

In his reinterpretations of Manet's paintings, Cézanne wavers between tribute and parody, just as his personal relationship with this modern master was marked by an inferiority complex concerning their social status on the one hand, and an openly derisive reaction to this supposed difference on the other. In any case, Cézanne had gained a reputation for his rebellious, provocatory stances and was determined to do Manet one better when it came to shocking the bourgeoisie. His *A Modern Olympia* (1869-70) is certainly not a faithful rendition of Manet's masterpiece, as it makes the latter's subtle implications quite explicit. Olympia is a prostitute and the setting is a brothel. In Cézanne's version, the woman's client is part of the scene and is clearly Cézanne himself. In a certain sense, the artist, not content with merely creating a variation of Manet's famous work, actually made himself a part of it. At the 1874 Salon another, smaller version of this subject aroused a scandal. And when Cézanne set out to make a 'modern' interpretation of Manet's *Déjeuner sur l'herbe* (1870-71), he chose a totally different, strange setting – the dim light of a stormy night, the dark tones of which again reveal his rejection of 'good painting.' Over and above the obvious scene of a gathering of friends, the scene is forced, almost ominous. A little fruit for a picnic, an empty bottle lying on the ground, the so-called

revellers frozen in carefully worked-out poses: one is sticking out a finger, another has her hand on her mouth, a man props up his cheek with his right hand while another one has his arms crossed. The figures are isolated, set in an artificially created landscape. The unmistakable, thoughtful figure of the artist in the foreground indicates that Cézanne is introducing a composition with hidden meanings and autobiographical references. We get the impression that Cézanne has reached a turning point, that this is a violent reaction that will lead him to a totally different conception of art. His passionate turmoil was about to be sublimated into its opposite, his emotional wellspring was to find a new equilibrium. Now a close friend of Pissarro, who was his greatest admirer, Cézanne achieved a concrete definition of the sensory reality that surrounded him; he embraced pictorial structures informed by logic and finality; he sought to understand and render his world through an objective, detached, impersonal approach, while still retaining all the vigour that had nurtured the metamorphoses of his art in the 1860s. In the still lifes executed after 1870 it would be useless to look for traces of the symbolic elements and precursory signs of Expressionism he had included in his 1866 still lifes (*Still Life with Skull and Candlestick*, *Still Life with Bread and Leg of Lamb*). The later works have the stamp of assurance and intimate grandeur that even Chardin does not possess. Until that time still lifes had been generally considered a rather predictable appendage of daily life; now they became a manifesto of an aesthetic, a hymn to the abundance and magnitude of life rendered through the stark, impersonal quality of everyday objects, capable of retaining their creator's wealth of emotion, over and above the total artistic autonomy of the forms he attained.

It would be interesting to try to re-create Cézanne's friends' and admirers' descriptions of his solemn and yet moving ritual in arranging the cloth, bottles and jugs for his still lifes – a secret rite to sublimate and exalt the banality of these objects. Besides the classical models, his still lifes drew

inspiration from Courbet and Manet; but while the latter was the poet of forms savoured through fine brushwork and distilled in their essence in light patterns, for Cézanne they were emblematic appearances that betokened a deeper level of consciousness, a sense of a universal order. "Aix is the driving force behind this obstinacy. Cézanne always works crudely, with all his strength, in order to rein in his temperament and impose the rules of a serene science. If he achieves his end we will soon be admiring fine and complex works," said Fortuné Marion.

An excellent example of Cézanne's pursuit of structural order is *Still Life with Green Pot and Pewter Jug* (1870), with the subtle contrasts and latent harmony he establishes among the objects. Roger Fry became convinced of the artist's greatness when he saw this canvas, while *Still Life with a Black Clock* (1870) had the same effect on the poet Rainer Maria Rilke. This profound painting, rich in references to his relations with Zola and enhanced by the open reddish shell with its disturbing erotic connotation, is rife with enigmatic symbols, such as the clock without hands. The canvas is vigorously structured by means of a play of accentuated vertical and horizontal movement that underscores the thick layers of pigment; it revolves around the contrast, and ultimate reconciliation, between the shape of the objects – so emotionally charged, since Cézanne was painting this still life for Zola – and the artist's detachment from the canvas to heighten the painterly values, the relationship between the volumes and the spatial organization. In 1872 he discovered in objectivity and order a sublimation of his love for violence and of the violence of his love. For the rest of his life he would struggle against his 'demons'; he realized that he could attain his new-found artistic goals only by openly addressing his inner conflicts and torments. He went to Paris at the end of year. In Guillaumin's atelier he executed a tormented self-portrait with the last flames of his unbridled passion, which were then quenched in the canvases of the years immediately following.

38

♦ Spring, *1860-62.*
Oil on canvas,
314 × 97 cm
(123 5/8 × 38 1/4
in). Musée du Petit
Palais, Paris.

♦ Summer, *1860-62.*
Oil on canvas,
314 × 109 cm
(123 5/8 × 43 in).
Musée du Petit
Palais, Paris.

◆ Autumn, *1860-62.*
Oil on canvas,
314 × 104 cm
(123 5/8 × 41 in).
Musée du Petit
Palais, Paris.

◆ Winter, *1860-62.*
Oil on canvas,
314 × 104 cm
(123 5/8 × 41 in).
Musée du Petit
Palais, Paris.

40

♦ *Opposite:* Portrait of the Artist's Father, *1862. Oil on canvas, 167.5 × 114.3 cm (66 × 45 in). National Gallery, London. A powerful interpretation of contemporary realism, this portrait, influenced by the painting in the Spanish style of Courbet's followers, is rendered in an original and solid manner.*

♦ *Above:* Head of an Old Man, *c. 1865. Oil on canvas, 51 × 48 cm (20 × 18 7/8 in). Musée d'Orsay, Paris.*

42

♦ The Judgement
of Paris, 1862-64.
Oil on canvas,
15 × 21 cm
(6 × 8 1/4 in).
Private Collection.
This is one of
Cézanne's first
scenes with female
nudes in a natural
setting. The figures
are handled in
a summary fashion,
with a Venetian-type
colour range. The
work anticipates his
later compositions
of bathers, one of the
basic motifs of his
maturity.

♦ *Above:* Dante and Vergil in Hell (after Delacroix), *c. 1864. Oil on canvas, 25 × 33 cm (9 7/8 × 13 in). Private Collection, Cambridge. Delacroix inspired many young artists. Cézanne copied this work directly from the original at the Louvre, when the museum gave him permission to work there on 20 November 1863.*

♦ *Below:* Landscape near Aix-en-Provence, *c. 1865. Oil on canvas, 40 × 59 cm (15 3/4 × 23 1/4 in). Insel Hombroich. The style in this work is similar to that of Corot and the Barbizon school painters. The motif of foliage, summarily rendered in large, dark masses, stands out against the sky with its thick texture.*

44

♦ *Opposite above:*
House in Provence,
1865-67.
Watercolour,
21 × 34 cm
(8 1/4 × 13 3/8 in).
Cabinet des Dessins,
Musée du Louvre,
Paris.

♦ *Opposite below:*
Landscape, c. 1865.
Oil on canvas,
26 × 35 cm
(10 1/4 × 13 3/4 in).
Vassar College Art
Gallery,
Poughkeepsie, NY.

♦ *Above:* Still Life
with Bread and Eggs,
1865. Oil on canvas,
59 × 76 cm
(23 1/4 × 29 7/8 in).
Art Museum,
Cincinnati. A frugal
meal set against
a dark background
evokes the Spanish
still life tradition,
which was inspiring
some French
painters in this
period. Though some
scholars see
Courbet's influence
in this work, the
broad areas of
colour and thick
texture are closer
to Manet.

46

♦ *Above:* Still Life with Skull and Candlestick, *c. 1866. Oil on canvas, 47.5 × 62.5 cm (18 3/4 × 24 1/2 in). Private Collection (on loan to the Kunsthaus, Zurich). Cézanne's predilection for painting with a palette knife derived from Courbet. Unlike the impersonal style then in fashion that reduced the motif to a mere harmony of tones, this canvas is charged with symbolic content. Together with the* symbols of the Enlightenment, it represents the intense religious feeling of the processions in Aix, in which skulls played an important role. This work was executed for Heinrich Morstatt, the German musician who introduced his friends in Aix to Wagner's intoxicating, passionate music. As Cézanne wrote in 1865: "We let our nerves vibrate with the noble tones of Richard Wagner."

♦ *Opposite above:* Still Life with Sugar Bowl, Pears and Cup, *c. 1866. Oil on canvas, 30 × 41 cm (11 3/4 × 16 1/8 in). Musée d'Orsay, Paris (on loan to the Musée Granet, Aix-en-Provence). This canvas appears reproduced in Cézanne's portrait of his father reading "L'Événement." It reveals how the line draws its energy from the violent colour. The intensity in the modelling of the pears, cup, and sugar bowl was never surpassed in this period.*

♦ *Opposite below:* Still Life with Bread and Leg of Lamb, *c. 1866. Oil on canvas, 27 × 35 cm (10 5/8 × 13 3/4 in). Kunsthaus, Zurich. Subtle contrasts in style and subject and a mixture of delicacy and crudeness, are all part of the great still life tradition. In modelling the meat Cézanne conveys the solidity of sculpture and is not afraid to depict violence, which he considered part of human nature and which was a basic feature of his oeuvre in this period.*

48

♦ *Opposite above:* View of Bonnières, *1866. Oil on canvas, 38 × 61 cm (15 × 24 in). Musée Faure, Aix-les-Bains. This work is an example of the style Cézanne adopted in 1866: thick layers of pigment that create areas of colours which are more similar to Manet's smooth areas than Courbet's coarse-grained ones.*

♦ *Opposite below:* Self-portrait, *c. 1866. Oil on canvas, 45 × 41 cm (17 5/8 × 16 1/8 in). Private Collection. "Paul is wonderful this year with his thin and extremely long hair and revolutionary beard," Fortuné Marion wrote to Morstatt in August 1866.*

♦ *Above:* Portrait of Anthony Valabrègue, *1866; 116.3 × 98.4 cm (45 3/4 × 38 3/4 in). National Gallery of Art, Washington, DC. This is the first of three portraits of his childhood friend. Cézanne sent it to the 1866 Salon as an act of provocation, since the artist certainly had no illusions of being accepted. This was the year in which the palette knife became a regular part of his pictorial procedure, and this portrait of his writer friend represents one of the first stages of this development. When he did not use the palette knife he applied the paint with dabs of the brush set one over the other in an attempt to enhance the tonal values.*

50

♦ *Above*: Portrait of the Artist's Father Reading "L'Événement," *1866. Oil on canvas, 198.5 × 119.3 cm (78 1/8 × 47 in). National Gallery of Art, Washington, DC. This portrait is an intimate Impressionist domestic scene which, like the contemporary works by Manet, Monet, Renoir, and Degas, was large-sized so it could be submitted to the Salon.*

♦ *Opposite above:* Uncle Dominique (The Jurist), *c. 1866. Oil on canvas, 63 × 52 cm (24 7/8 × 20 7/16 in). Musée d'Orsay, Paris.*

♦ *Opposite below:* Uncle Dominique in Profile, *1866. Oil on canvas, 39 × 30.5 cm (15 3/8 × 12 in). King's College, Cambridge (on loan to the Fitzwilliam Museum, Cambridge).*

52

♦ *Above:* Man with Cotton Cap (Uncle Dominique), *1866. Oil on canvas, 84 × 64 cm (33 × 25 1/8 in). Metropolitan Museum of Art, New York. Like Fragonard's 'fantasy figures' or Daumier's caricatures, Cézanne's portraits of Uncle Dominique tell us more about the artist's ideas concerning social classes than about the personality of the subject portrayed.*

♦ *Opposite:* Portrait of Uncle Dominique as a Monk, *c. 1866 Oil on canvas, 65 × 54 cm (25 1/2 × 21 1/4 in). Walter Annenberg Collection, Palm Springs. Cézanne's harsh, impetuous, violent handling is accentuated by his use of the palette knife. Within the context of the intensely wrought material properties, the space acquires its very own structure and rhythm.*

54

♦ Portrait of the
Artist's Mother,
1866-67. Oil on
canvas, 53 × 37 cm
(20 7/8 × 14 9/16 in).
St. Louis Art
Museum, St. Louis.
Cézanne painted
this work on the
back of a portrait of
his sister Marie. For
a long time it was
hidden under a thick
layer of black paint
and was discovered
after being
purchased by the St.
Louis Art Museum.

♦ Portrait of the Artist's Sister Marie, 1866-67. Oil on canvas, 55 × 38 cm (21 5/8 × 15 in). St. Louis Art Museum, St. Louis. Cézanne effects the delicacy and vibrancy of the face by broadly applying the pigment with a palette knife, while the background, shoulders and chest are rendered through linear bands of colour that seem to have been applied haphazardly, as if to correct or even annul the drawing. The artist was moving away from his so-called 'couillarde style' towards a more fluid and linear one that would later become markedly rhythmic as well.

56

♦ Mary Magdalene (Sorrow), c. 1867. *Oil on canvas, 165 × 124 cm (65 × 48 3/4 in). Musée d'Orsay, Paris. After Cézanne's death this painting, along with others, was removed from the salon at the* *Jas de Bouffan in 1907 and separated from* Christ in Limbo *– with which it formed a single work – because of the stylistic differences between the two parts. The artist drew inspiration from* *Domenico Fetti's* Melancholy *at the Louvre and perhaps from a small work by Pierre Subleyras kept at the Granet Museum in Aix. There have been various interpretations of this rather* *ambiguous work; some critics consider the juxtaposition of Christ and Magdalene a traditional Easter subject, while others interpret the painting in a secular key.*

♦ The Negro Scipio, c. 1867. Oil on canvas, 107 × 83 cm (42 1/8 × 32 5/8 in). Museu de Arte, São Paulo. The figure portrayed was a model at the Académie Suisse, where Cézanne often worked from 1862 on. The image is analogous to the dark figure of the abductor in The Rape; the impetuosity of the sinuous, upward-moving brushstrokes is balanced by the inertia of the stripes of colour that move downwards. Here Cézanne's use of rhythmic brushwork is at its height, and the solid masses of impasto of 1866 give way to what would seem to be the opposite principle in his art. This work belonged to Monet, who called it a "piece of primeval power" and kept it in his bedroom with the other favourite paintings in his collection.

58

♦ An Afternoon in
Naples, 1866-67.
Oil on canvas,
37 × 45 cm
(14 5/8 × 17 3/4 in).
Australian National
Gallery, Canberra.
This may be one
of the canvases on
drunkenness that
were rejected at the
1867 Salon. The
bizarre title was
suggested
to Cézanne by
G.-B.-A. Guillaumin.
The controversial
theme is rendered
with scurrilous
relish, obviously
with the aim of
scandalizing and
of refuting the
common notion
whereby a great
painter must always
create works of good
taste.

♦ *Above:* Study for 'The Autopsy," *1867-69. Charcoal, 31 × 48 cm (11 1/2 × 18 7/8 in). Art Institute, Chicago.*

♦ *Below:* The Autopsy (Preparation for a Funeral), *1867-69. Oil on canvas, 49 × 80 cm (19 1/4 × 31 1/2 in). Galerie Beyeler, Basle.*

60

♦ *Above:* Rue des Saules in Montmartre, *c. 1867. Oil on canvas, 32 × 41 cm (12 3/8 × 16 1/8 in). Private Collection. Cézanne replaced the palette knife with a technique of sharp strokes with a large brush that allowed him to paint a landscape he probably would not have been able to render with the sinuous brushwork he had previously adopted. This intense and spontaneous work is in some ways an anticipation of Expressionism.*

♦ *Opposite above:* The Rape (The Abduction), *c. 1867. Oil on canvas, 90.5 × 117 cm (35 1/2 × 46 in). King's College, Cambridge (on loan to the Fitzwilliam Museum, Cambridge). Cézanne executed this work for Zola in his house at Rue de la Condamine. Some critics have connected the motif to certain romantic writings by the young author, but Mary Tompkins Lewis affirms it is a representation of Pluto abducting Proserpina. The* landscape, a shadowy valley, and the 'scenographic' elements of the drama are organized much like the setting in a canvas by Niccolò dell'Abate at the Louvre. Mont Sainte-Victoire is in the background instead of Mt. Etna. The composition is part of a tradition that ranges from Tintoretto to Daumier, but the controlled refulgence of the colour paved the way for new horizons in his pictorial procedure.

♦ *Opposite below:* Women Dressing, *c. 1867. Oil on paper glued to canvas, 22 × 32 cm (8 5/8 × 13 3/8 in). Insel Hombroich. A distant memory of idyllic scenes in the Millet manner, this work was given to Pissarro as a present. It marks Cézanne's first experimentation with the brilliant, original colour that would reach its peak in* The Rape.

62

♦ Portrait of Achille Emperaire, *1868-70.* *Oil on canvas, 200 × 122 cm (78 3/4 × 48 in). Musée d'Orsay, Paris. The armchair is the same one Cézanne used for the famous portrait of* his father, but the two works are quite different. The Impressionist nuances are here replaced by vigorous, schematic drawing. The distinct areas of colour permit the *artist to render the outlines clearly, each surface area is a well defined and independent unit. At the time, Cézanne had exploited his talent for draughtsmanship to the full.*

♦ Head of Achille Emperaire, *1868-70.* *Charcoal and pencil, 49 × 31 cm (19 1/4 × 11 1/2 in). Cabinet des Dessins, Musée du Louvre, Paris.*

● Curving Road in
Provence, c. 1868.
Oil on canvas,
91 × 71 cm
(35 7/8 × 28 in).
Museum of Fine
Arts, Montreal.
Around the end
of the 1860s

Cézanne began
to set thickly
impastoed areas of
colours next to one
another, a technique
he would take up
again in the first
winter he spent
at Auvers.

64

♦ *Above:* A Modern Olympia, *1869-70, oil on canvas, 56 × 55.5 cm (22 × 21 7/8 in). Private Collection.* Cézanne drew upon Manet's famous work, setting the subject in a more 'modern' context. This may be a tribute to the recognized master of the modern style, or perhaps Cézanne intended to provoke Manet, as he did in real life. In any case, it is not a faithful rendering of Manet's composition but rather an explicit translation of his allusions. Olympia is a prostitute and the setting is a brothel. The observer, who is merely suggested in Manet's painting, is Cézanne himself.

♦ *Opposite above:* The Overture to Tannhäuser, *1860-70. Oil on canvas, 57 × 92 cm (22 1/2 × 36 1/4 in). Hermitage Museum, St. Petersburg.* In 1937 Alfred Barr identified the subject on the basis of some letters of Fortuné Marion, Cézanne's childhood friend, to the young German musician Heinrich Morstatt.

♦ *Opposite below:* Contrasts, *1869-70. Oil on canvas, 50 × 40 cm (19 5/8 × 15 3/4 in). The Ian Woodner Family Collection.* The brushwork is reminiscent of Daumier, while the man's head shows the influence of Courbet. Originally, this work decorated the salon wall in the Jas de Bouffan.

66

♦ *Above:* Skull and Jug, *1868-70. Oil on canvas, 60 × 50 cm (23 5/8 × 19 5/8 in). Private Collection. "He once painted on a warm, dark, impastoed canvas, pathetic as a Rembrandt, a skull on a crumpled towel in front of a jug of milk, as if it had just emerged from the depths of God knows what sepulchral cave or from out of the blue. I still remember him reciting a verse from Verlaine one evening: 'In this lethargic world / eternally prey to old regrets / the only logical laughter / is that of the heads of the dead.'" (Joaquim Gasquet).*

♦ *Opposite above:* The Thieves and the Ass, *1869-70. Oil on canvas, 41 × 55 cm (16 1/8 × 21 5/8 in). Civiche Raccolte d'Arte, Milan. This painting illustrates Apeleius's* Golden Ass *in a light-handed, Daumier-like baroque style – an unusual comic motif for Cézanne.*

♦ *Opposite below:* Paul Alexis Reading to Zola, *c. 1868-69. Oil on canvas, 52 × 56 cm (20 7/16 × 22 in). Private Collection, Switzerland. In a dim atmosphere, Paul Alexis reads a manuscript to Émile Zola, who listens with his back to the spectator.*

68

♦ Factories in front of the Mont du Cengle, 1869-70. Oil on canvas, 41 × 55 cm (16 1/8 × 21 5/8 in). Private Collection. This is an imaginary industrial landscape that was part of a series Cézanne executed by recalling the countryside near Aix and L'Estaque. The series is characterized by thick impasto, a concise and sometimes (but not in this case) apocalyptic atmosphere. The industrial setting also interested Guillaumin and Pissarro in this period and was adopted by Zola in his novels.

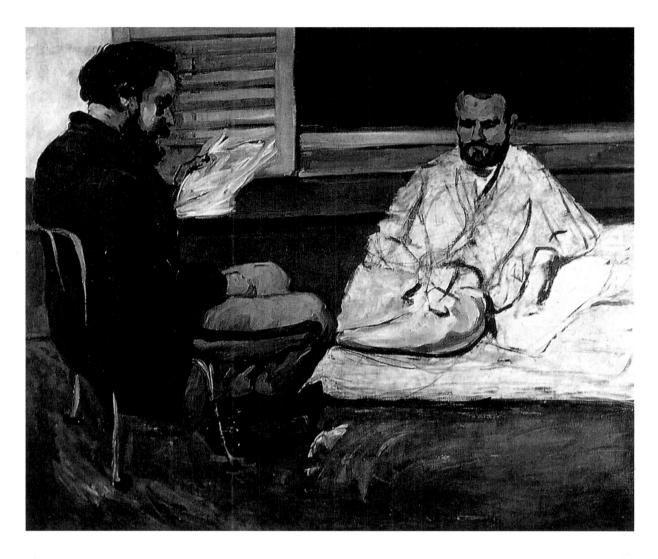

♦ *Above:* Paul Alexis Reads a Manuscript to Émile Zola, *1869-70. Oil on canvas, 131 × 161 cm (51 1/2 × 63 3/8 in). Museu de Arte, São Paulo. This is another large, mysterious and fascinating version of the theme of the* intellectual and work companionship of Zola and Alexis. Zola's unusual pose, more suitable for an odalisque than a realistic novelist, and his passive role as a listener, refer to certain character traits of his. In 1868 *the Goncourt brothers asserted that he seemed younger than he really was, had delicate features and "an ambiguous, almost hermaphroditic physique," in which the feminine features dominated.*

♦ *Below:* The Dance, *1869-71. Pencil, 12 × 22 cm (4 3/4 × 8 5/8 in). Graphische Sammlung Albertina, Vienna.*

♦ Pastoral (or Idyll), c. 1870. Oil on canvas, 65 × 81 cm (25 1/2 × 31 7/8 in). Musée d'Orsay, Paris. This canvas belongs to the group, executed around 1870, with an outdoor, pastoral setting, and is based on Manet's Déjeuner sur l'herbe. But Cézanne transforms the latter's realistic rendering into an imaginative, dream-like, slightly ominous scene filled with erotic symbolism expressed not only in the figures but also in nature itself – the voluptuous convolutions of the trees and clouds, the reflections on the water, and even the relationship between the bottle and glass, which represent a human couple. The dynamic rendering of the landscape in vaguely human shapes was quite rare in the painting of the time.

♦ The Feast (or
The Orgy), c. 1870.
Oil on canvas.
130 × 81 cm
(51 1/8 × 31 7/8 in).
Private Collection,
Switzerland.
The scene was
inspired by
a passage from
Flaubert's The
Temptation of St.
Anthony. *Cézanne's
image is perfectly
in keeping with
the description
of Nebuchadezzar's
banquet in the
second version
of Flaubert's work,
which was
published in serial
form in "L'Artiste"
in 1856-57.*

72

♦ *Opposite above:*
Still Life with Green
Pot and Pewter Jug,
1870. Oil on canvas,
63 × 80 cm
(24 7/8 × 31 1/2 in).
Musée d'Orsay,
Paris. Cézanne here
meditates on latent
harmonies and
subtle contrasts
among the silent
objects. The canvas,
executed between
the end of his early
period and the
beginning of his
artistic maturity,
condenses the
gloomy strength and
concentrated energy
typical of his early
paintings.

♦ *Opposite below:*
Still Life with a Black
Clock, *c. 1870*
Oil on canvas,
55.2 × 74.3 cm
(21 3/4 × 29 1/4 in).
Niarchos Collection,
Paris. This work
marks a
breakthrough in
Cézanne's career
and is proof of his
mastery of this
subject. The
composition is
tightly organized
by means of a play
of vertical and
horizontal accents
that contrast with
the shapes of the
lemon, shell, cup,
vase and inkwell,

objects he would
never again paint
and perhaps
containing hidden
meanings, since
Cézanne executed
this still life for
Zola. The palette
resembles Manet's –
his blacks, greys and
whites, and the
intense yellows.
The clock without
hands symbolizes
timelessness, in
keeping with the
aesthetic-
contemplative
character of the
work.

♦ *Above:* Still Life
with Pot, Bottle, Cup
and Fruit, *c. 1871.*
Oil on canvas,
64 × 80 cm
(25 1/8 × 31 1/2 in).
Nationalgalerie der
Staatliche Museen,
Berlin. The fact that
common household
objects had such
a revolutionary
impact on the
contents and form
of Western art is
nothing less than
a miracle. Cézanne
dedicated himself
utterly to the logical,
monumental
construction in the
quest for absolute
values.

74

♦ The Railway
Cutting, c. 1870.
Oil on canvas,
80 × 129 cm
(31 1/2 × 50 7/8 in).
Neue Pinakothek,
Munich. This work
marked an
important stage in
Cézanne's artistic
development; he
began to abandon
his violent pictorial
handling and to
study nature and its
laws. Although his
palette was still
based on strong
chiaroscuro
contrasts and earthy
tones, he was
brightening it.
His composition
now became
monumental, and
for the most part did
away with depth;
the different planes
are now parallel and
seem to converge at
the middle of the
canvas. The railway
cutting in this work
begins from an old
house on the hill,
with Sainte-Victoire
at right. The
landscape has no
human presence, and
the deep wound in
the earth corresponds
rhythmically to the
mountain
dominating a
horizon that suggests
the sea. The various
elements in this
canvas are invested
with deep meaning
by the stark
construction and
converging
viewpoint, and
bespeak the heroism
of solitude and the
quest for the
permanent essence of
nature in the midst
of the changes
effected by man.

◆ Melting Snow
at L'Estaque, c. 1870.
Oil on canvas,
73 × 92 cm
(28 3/4 × 36 1/4 in).
E.G. Bührle
Foundation, Zurich.
In this composition,
with its sharp colour
contrasts, dramatic
dialogue between
black and white,
deliberately
summary drawing,
and dynamic,
turbulent forms,
Cézanne set out to
render immediate a
sensation of great
intensity, a
vehement, almost
illogical impression.
In the foreground the
steep side of a hill
divides the surface
of the canvas
diagonally, creating
a falling sensation
with the trees
holding on to the
unstable earth with
their convoluted
trunks. Parallel and
diagonal lines
delimit opposing
tensions. Cézanne
here discovers the
drama of space and
renders it in terms
of powerful
movements and
sudden contrasts
in an overwhelming
perspective. The bold
colours and
brushwork incarnate
the vehemence of the
scene. A darkish hue
permeates the entire
landscape, lending it
an air of melancholy
and solitude despite
the occasional subtle
flashes of colour.
Manet's impassive
elegance in his use
of whites, blacks and
greys is here altered
in a strikingly
passionate manner.

76

♦ *Opposite above:*
Landscape with
Water Mill, *c. 1871*
Oil on canvas,
41 × 54 cm
(16 1/8 × 21 1/4 in).
Yale University Art
Gallery, New Haven.

♦ *Opposite below:*
Avenue at the Jas
de Bouffan, *c. 1869.*
Oil on canvas,
38 × 46 cm
(15 × 18 1/8 in).
Tate Gallery,
London.

The newfound
stability in
Cézanne's
landscapes is clearly
seen here.

♦ *Above:* The Road,
c. 1871.
Oil on canvas,
59 × 72 cm
(23 1/4 × 23 3/8 in).
Private Collection,
USA.

♦ *Above:* Venus and
Cupid, *1870-73.*
Oil on canvas,
21 × 21 cm
(8 1/4 × 8 1/4 in).
Private Collection,
Tokyo.

♦ *Opposite above:*
The Temptation
of St. Anthony, *1870.*
Oil on canvas,
54 × 73 cm
(21 1/4 × 28 3/4 in).
E.G. Bührle

Foundation, Zurich.
This is the first
of Cézanne's several
versions of
Flaubert's theme.

♦ *Opposite below:* Le
déjeuner sur l'herbe,
1870-71.
Oil on canvas,
60 × 80 cm
(23 5/8 × 31 1/2 in).
Private Collection.

80

♦ The Strangled
Woman, c. 1872.
Oil on canvas,
31 × 15 cm
(11 1/2 × 6 in).
Musée d'Orsay,
Paris. A scene

of violence and death
betrays the artist's
passionate
temperament and his
obsession with the
struggle between man
and woman.

♦ The Walk, *c. 1871.*
Oil on canvas,
58 × 46 cm
(22 7/8 × 18 1/8 in).
Charles Payson

Collection, New York.
This work was copied
faithfully from
an 1871 magazine
illustration.

82

♦ Portrait of Anthony Valabrègue, c. 1871. Oil on canvas, 60.3 × 50.1 cm (23 3/4 × 19 3/4 in). J. Paul Getty Museum, Malibu. This canvas is a brilliant demonstration of Cézanne's artistic maturity, rendered with even more vigour and surety than in his portraits of his uncle Dominique. What perhaps strikes one most here is the expression Cézanne captures or imagines in his friends – as if the disappointments that affected the generation that witnessed the disastrous effects of the war had sparked in these still young men the urge to prove their worth in order to restore the true values of human existence.

♦ Man with a Straw Hat (Gustave Boyer), c. 1871. Oil on canvas, 55 × 39 cm (21 5/8 × 15 3/8 in). Metropolitan Museum of Art, New York. Cézanne here gives his childhood friend the features of a provincial character in a Balzac novel – ambitious and determined. The energy that exudes from this canvas stems from the artist's vigorous pictorial handling, which is expressed in the robust forms and strong colours. The figure conveys grim determination, manifested in the brushstrokes: Cézanne applies both thin and thick layers of paint, carefully models the facial features and chooses the tones, blending the warm surface of the hat with the face surrounded by black and utilizing greys and neutral hues with subtlety and surety.

♦ Self-portrait,
1873-76. Oil on
canvas, 64 × 53 cm
(25 1/8 × 20 7/8 in).
Musée d'Orsay,
Paris This image
expresses the
enthusiasm of a
human being who
has just awakened
from a nightmare
of solitude and
sexual frustration
in order to reconcile
himself with life.

This turning-point
in Cézanne's life
stemmed not only
from his liaison
with Hortense,
his friendship
with the "humble
and colossal"
Pissarro, and his
faithfulness to the
truth of his
sensations, but also
from his awareness
of, and belief in,
his greatness.

The Truth of Plein-air Painting

When he went to live in Pontoise in 1872, Cézanne took up plein-air painting under Pissarro's guidance. His life had taken a turn for the better. He had sublimated his rage, become more sociable and opened his heart to natural beauty. He now adopted the technique of brief brushstrokes, abandoned drawing for gradations of colour and brightened his palette, thus embarking on the intense and monumental labour of reshaping Impressionist pictorial procedure. As a disciple of Corot, therefore an artist who paid particular attention to the form of objects as well as to the coloured atmosphere of light reflections, Pissarro did not completely agree with the Impressionists' predilection for the ephemeral effects of sense perception. A certain solidity and quest for balance had always been an integral part of his style. Now this generous artist instilled in Cézanne both discipline in rendering nature and the joy of light and colour.

Around 1870, in seclusion at L'Estaque, Cézanne felt the need for a more intimate relationship with nature. Such canvases as *Melting Snow at L'Estaque* were still based on dramatic colour schemes that were worlds apart from the light Impressionist touch. His desire for fresh contact with the world became quite apparent in 1872. He initiated that process of detachment and objective analysis through which the various elements of the canvas were no longer at odds but were merged in an all-embracing visual synthesis. Now light determined the development of spatial planes and lent substance to the colour with its penetrating vibrations. The canvases Cézanne executed in Pontoise and Auvers-sur-Oise reveal his fecund rapport with Impressionism – but he replaced the Impressionist atmosphere with a rendering of forms by means of built-up dabs of colour, a sign that his vision of perception aimed at establishing the consistency of reality side by side with its eternal becoming. Pissarro gave Cézanne the opportunity to keep his temperament under control through new pictorial procedures. He began to use colour as a primary means of creating a unified atmosphere and tightening the composition as well as of lending a different consistency to the various objects. Bright colours now took the place of conventional hues and the sudden transitions from light to dark areas he had formerly used to model shapes and create dramatic effects. By adopting the Impressionist technique, his painting became more specifically visual and was freed from the shackles of imaginative motifs without, however, losing any of the necessary stylistic vigour.

Cézanne was now totally receptive to the fascination of nature. He diluted the strong contrasts by creating softer harmonies; his brushwork, which had formerly had a broad, impetuous rhythm, now rendered his sensations in a more orderly and deliberate fashion. He drew inspiration more from the outside world than from his inner self. The large areas were divided or interrupted by brief brushstrokes and the overall composition kept his dramatic impulses in check, becoming in the process more detailed thanks to the greater variety of colours. His works were now informed by greater freedom and a new-found tranquillity. The early style gave way to the penetrating power of outdoor painting, which he exploited to the utmost.

The masterpiece of Cézanne's first Impressionist years is *The House of the Hanged Man* (c. 1873), an unusual, fantastic view that even in the title suggests the artist's propensity for disturbing motifs. An invisible tragedy has unfolded in a place that still emanates an air of death, darkness and absence. But the ambiguity and mystery of the canvas dissolve in the golden late afternoon light under a clear sky. Cézanne captures the quality of the different material properties of the painting, enhancing their characteristics and complexity. The sky takes up very little surface area, is circumscribed as it were, and even the light seems to be solidified. The geological character of the elements is respected to the utmost. This is a powerful image, not only because of the sober colours, which are rich in the middle range, but above all because of Cézanne's conception of the scene and the vigour of the tightly structured, densely packed composition. The relationship between the houses and rocks with their similar shapes; the unstable, steeply descending earth; the complicated, indirect line of vision into the depths of the landscape; the panorama and horizon confined within a narrow space – all create a space marked by conflict so different from the open, mobile and indistinct space of Impressionist painting. Cézanne's predilection for radical viewpoints, abrupt contrasts and difficult transitions give rise to oblique lines, diagonal axes and breaks that underscore the uniqueness of the structure.

In *Study: Landscape at Auvers* (1873), his attraction for light and colour overwhelm the solid, concentrated structure. Marked off by houses, trees and fields, the landscape extends in different directions without offering the observer any specific line of vision. This is an example of an utterly new, vital relationship with nature – though in certain touches on the walls, the leaves or the roofs, we clearly see Cézanne's resolutely structural vision. The fascination of light and colour also dominates in *View of Auvers* (1873). The strongest colours – blue, red and white – are applied in small, scattered patches, and the white both brightens and softens the whole. Depth is created here by the overlaid elements moving off into the distance and becoming smaller and smaller. The intensity of the colours and the contrast among corresponding tonalities change through the brief caesurae between the foreground and the horizon. Colour distribution ranges from the relative chaos of the foreground and the middle section to the clarity of the distant planes. The surfaces give the impression of a loosely structured, variegated and yet homogeneous aggregate.

This was the period in which nature and painting were celebrated in the same luminous and serene clarity that betoken a rare moment of *joie de vivre* and felicitous creation in Cézanne's career. The landscape and light of Auvers and Pontoise are different from those in Provence, and Pissarro's example and gift for observation transformed Cézanne's palette. Working outdoors among the objects in their natural setting, he broadened his vision of the world without in the least undermining his quest for stability, orderly structure and unity. The factor of permanence was as important as space for him; just as he used atmosphere as a structural element, he also painted with the idea of capturing the eternal essence of things.

In the most famous canvases in this period – *The House of Père Lacroix* and the three versions of *The House of Dr. Gachet*, with the effects produced by the snow in the vicinity of Auvers and the winding country roads flanked by trees and houses – Cézanne dispenses with flashing, vaporous light and does not dilute the landscape in chromatic iridescence in which the very substance of things dissolve. The trees are rendered as solidly as the houses; the sky and clouds are affected by the vibrations of the wind and light, but despite these fleeting transmutations still maintain the sense of the permanence and immutability of being, the most intimate essence of which cannot be changed.

In the mid-1870s Cézanne began working with parallel brushstrokes to express visual sensations by means of patches of coloured light so as to attain greater definition of space. Pissarro, who worked with his friend outdoors, also began to adopt a richer brushstroke that lent a new meaning to space, and it was perhaps his relationship with Cézanne that brought about the artistic crisis he underwent in the latter part of the decade.

Cézanne added a new dimension to the luminous vision of his artist friends which stemmed from his efforts to clarify and harmonize two apparently irreconcilable extremes. If we consider the fluid, luminous vision of the world created in the canvases of this period, Cézanne could be called an Impressionist; but in his oeuvre a different, subtle tension is always present, making his painting more complex and meaningful, albeit less popular.

Besides landscapes, he executed portraits, self-portraits, and still lifes. He also painted purely imaginative canvases that were not based on objective perception and that confirm his absolutely unique position in the Impressionist group. He shared his friends' great adventure of freeing colour through light, but continued to create those strange symbolic and erotic scenes that have little in common with optical realism and the dissolution of forms in the splendour of atmospheric effects. These motifs were often cumbersome for Cézanne and he found it difficult to represent female nudes (which were sometimes rendered awkwardly or poorly) because of his inability to realize a desire that could not be expressed in painting; moreover, one notes defiance, derision and even brutality that are signs of sincerity and vitality.

Compared to similar works of the 1830s, Cézanne here has a lighter, more vibrant brushstroke and impasto which reflect, albeit indirectly, his plein-air experience. He continued his 'dialogue' with Manet with new versions of *A Modern Olympia*, *Le déjeuner sur l'herbe*, *An Afternoon in Naples* and executed the Flaubertian motif of *The Temptation of St. Anthony* as well as *The Eternal Feminine* and *The Battle of Love*, canvases connected to his first studies for his *Bathers* which herald the later large-scale compositions on the same theme. *A Modern Olympia* (1873), executed for Gachet and shown at the first Impressionist exhibition, is more airy and less modelled than the preceding version, while maintaining its erotic and autobiographical features. With the impetuosity of a disciple of Fragonard, he put his newly acquired brushwork technique to good use, almost sketching rather than painting this scene with a rapid, nervous brushstroke that produces bright and lively colour effects. The oblique perspective creates an amazing breadth that uncovers, before the veil held up by a black woman, a nude woman lying on a white cloud, an empty space separating her from the seated man who is observing her. The overall effect is playful, sarcastic and provocatory.

The last work alluding to Manet is *An Afternoon in Naples*, of which Cézanne did several versions both in oils and watercolour from 1865 to 1875. Here again the brushwork and splendid palette reflect the artist's Impressionist experience. Delacroix's influence can be seen here, especially his *Women of Algiers*, but the poses, which are no longer indolent, reflect Cézanne's aggressive erotic conception.

The motif of seduction is recapitulated in *The Eternal Feminine*. A rather pale, flaccid and almost faceless Eve dominates the scene from her large canopied bed, at the foot of which are her admirers: painters, sculptors, musicians, bankers and even a bishop with his mitre and crosier. They are all worshipping the desired object of sin, and the scene is rather ambiguous, with an air of a sarcastic mirage or nightmare. Courbet's *The Artist's Studio* comes to mind here, while the 'guests' may be a literary reference to Apuleius's *The Golden Ass*. But Baudelaire's 'demonic woman' and Goethe's 'eternal feminine' are rendered in a grotesque vision in which Cézanne's personal obsessions are combined with caustic social criticism. The men gathered around the idol may represent the vices, materialism and hypocrisy of the bourgeoisie, and in this sense Cézanne himself is tempted by desire and guilty of unconfessable sins.

Although it was inspired both by the Venetians and Poussin, *The Battle of Love* transforms the spirit of the classical bacchanal into a scene of violence and rape. This brutal fantasy is expressed in a sort of uninterrupted dance – entwined bodies rolling on the ground and in the clouds, amidst the trees shaking in the wind – that permeates all of nature with its unbridled energy.

In the same period Cézanne sketched an *Apotheosis of Delacroix* with Pissarro, Monet, Choquet, an unidentified man, Cézanne himself and a dog paying tribute to the beloved painter. It is obvious how hard it was for an artist who felt the need to include symbols, autobiographical references and allusions to his inner torment in his works, to adapt to the lightness and thematic spontaneity of Impressionism. In a more tranquil and harmonious canvas dominated by a symphony of yellows and greens – one of the first great compositions with bathers, kept at the Metropolitan Museum in New York – there are six female nudes in an ethereal bucolic scene dominated by a strange tree in the form of a cross in the background. The first bathers Cézanne drew in a letter to Zola in 1859 are the three inseparable friends under a large tree; a later drawing, *Nudes in a Landscape* (1864-67), is a link between the violent erotic scenes of the late 1860s and the later nude bathers immersed in a natural setting. An 1870 canvas with bathers belonging to a private collection in Paris has both male and female nudes near a body of water, but from then on the artist's pastoral canvases and scenes of temptation would take different paths.

Bathers in Repose (1874-76, Barnes Foundation) is connected to Manet's *Déjeuner sur l'herbe* (which was originally titled *Le bain*), even though it is somewhat removed from the latter: Manet's figures are grouped harmoniously in an arch, while each of Cézanne's nudes goes his own way. Again, the forms and even the possible connotations vary: the trees are focal points that take on a figurative meaning, and the persons hiding behind them convey the idea of voyeurism. Together with the nude and the serpent, the image of the tree refers to temptation and original sin and is indirectly connected to Cézanne's apples. His nudes break away from the bathing ritual and gradually become enigmatic and universal figures.

Cézanne put his Impressionist experience to good use in his portraits, though he preserved the monumental character typical of his early works in this genre. His careful, detached observation is translated into refinement of procedure. *Madame Cézanne in a Red Armchair* (1877) is an architectural structure in which the play of patches of coloured light injects life into the portrait. In his self-portraits the strong, detached face with a touch of melancholy reveals – over and above the masterful handling of the material properties – a breath of inner truth.

Cézanne took part in the third Impressionist exhibition (1877), presenting landscapes, still lifes and the famous *Portrait of Victor Chocquet* with its thick, lumpy layers of paint applied with a technique that seemed arbitrary and scandalous to the public. After having acquired a sense of formal organization in the 1860s, Cézanne penetrated form with light, he linked and harmonized the various surface areas by means of subtle transitions and nuances that were a celebration of painting in its vivid, organic becoming.

That same year Édmond Duranty discussed the features of the Impressionist movement in *La nouvelle peinture* and analyzed its approach to colour: "As far as colouring is concerned, they have made a truly original discovery [...] it consists in the realization that a strong light discolours, that the sun, reflected by objects, tends by virtue of its brightness to give them this luminous unity by blending its seven prismatic rays into a single colourless brightness, which is light."

Already in 1876 Cézanne had written the interesting letter to Pissarro which shows how detached he really was from Impressionism. At L'Estaque he found that an analysis of light in its seven basic tones, as theorized by Duranty, could not be applied to the light of Provence nor to his painting, which perceived a bright, harsh colour in nature that could not be dissolved in light. "It's like a playing card," he said. "Red roofs over a blue sea." The imperative of structural volume is set against the mobility and ephemeral nature of Impressionism. The power of the silhouettes he perceived in nature was by then wholly antithetical to the objects dissolved in light common to his friends' pictorial procedure.

In Provence, the severe beauty of nature was the perfect expression of Cézanne's temperament; the 'terrifying' light reflected on objects accentuated their volume and led the artist to take another crucial step in his art. Without rejecting the Impressionist experience, he let himself be governed by his desire for structural logic, which was already noticeable in his earlier production and would assert itself more and more.

86

♦ *Above:* A Modern Olympia, *1872-73. Oil on canvas, 46 × 55.5 cm (18 1/8 × 21 7/8 in). Musée d'Orsay, Paris. This is the second version of the motif inspired by Manet's famous canvas. It is even more explicit in its denunciation of the commercialization of human relationships, a theme that was also described by Zola* in his novel Nana. *Cézanne executed this work when he was a guest at Dr. Gachet's house at Auvers. The handling of the motif is bold and brilliant; the contrast between the nudity of the woman and the clothing of the man in black and the silhouette of the little dog lend an intense erotic, theatrical tone to the canvas.*

♦ *Right:* The Village Road (Auvers), *1872-74. Oil on canvas, 46 × 55.5 cm (18 1/8 × 21 7/8 in). Musée d'Orsay, Paris. While at Auvers, Cézanne loved to paint its curving roads, scattered houses and bare trees. He succeeded in imparting expressive profundity even to the most common scene. To a certain* extent he adopted the Impressionist technique and palette, but he retained the structural density and complex perception of the sensory world that distinguished him from the freer, more objective 'eye' of his fellow artists. For him, Impressionist colour and technique were a point of departure for a new conception of art.

88

♦ *Above:* The House
of Dr. Gachet at
Auvers, *1873.*
Oil on canvas,
56 × 46 cm
(22 × 18 1/8 in).
Kunstmuseum,
Basle.

♦ *Opposite:* The
House of Dr. Gachet,
1873. Oil on canvas,
46 × 38 cm
(18 1/8 × 15 in).
Musée d'Orsay,
Paris.

90

♦ *Opposite:* The
House of Père
Lacroix, *1873.*
Oil on canvas,
61.5 × 51 cm
(24 1/4 × 20 in).
National Gallery
of Art, Washington,
DC. Painting
outdoors together
with Pissarro,
Cézanne tried to
capture the true
forms, colours and
spaces of the motif.
His procedure was
now more subdued
and he discarded
the passionate
impetuosity of his
preceding works.
His painting now
had more technique,
and perhaps less
originality.

♦ *Above:* The Rue
Rémy Junction
at Auvers, *1873.*
Oil on canvas,
38 × 45.5 cm
(15 × 18 in).
Musée d'Orsay,
Paris. Like The
House of the Hanged
Man, *but to a lesser*
extent, this canvas
is organized around
a complex structure
of planes that are
all seen from
multiple viewpoints.

92

♦ *Above:* The House
of the Hanged Man,
c. 1873.
Oil on canvas,
55 × 66 cm
(21 5/8 × 26 in).
Musée d'Orsay,
Paris.
This is considered
Cézanne's most
important painting
of the period. The
cold light of Île de
France, the use of
light colours even in
the shadows, and the
short brushstrokes,
are features that
can be found in the
contemporary works
of Monet, Pissarro
and Sisley. But what
for these artists
was the search for
spontaneity, was
for Cézanne the
conscious quest for
discipline as well as
the abandonment
of his preceding
style. This canvas,
together with the
others he executed
outdoors at Auvers,
marks a break,
a crucial turning-
point in both motifs
and technique;
yet it cannot be
wholly associated
with the typical
Impressionist
production, since
Cézanne's
composition is
rigorously
organized around
a central point of
view from which
oblique lines
radiate, and the
edges of the roofs,
walls, and slopes
make up a series
of triangles that are
linked with great
precision.

♦ *Opposite:* View
of Auvers, *c. 1873.*
Oil on canvas,
44.5 × 34.5 cm
(17 1/2 × 13 5/8 in).
Nathan L. Halpern
Collection.
With a harmony
of light colours and
very free brushwork,
Cézanne celebrates
both nature and
painting in this
luminous, serene
canvas. A series
of spots constitutes
the immaterial
tree in the
foreground.

94

♦ Study: Landscape at Auvers, *c. 1873.* *Oil on canvas, 47 × 52 cm (18 1/2 × 20 7/16 in). Museum of Art, Philadelphia.* *This work is the result of the profusion, delicacy and luminosity of its components. The depth is rendered not by converging lines, but by gradually receding planes. The tonalities are applied in no particular order, and the difference between the various hues of green is rendered with great sensitivity and subtlety. Cézanne uses only the primary colours and their immediate complementaries, and conveys – with acuteness and freshness – chromatic contrasts, the effects made by light, and the tones that change because of these effects.*

♦ The Outing (The
Pond), 1873-75.
Oil on canvas,
47 × 56 cm
(18 1/2 × 22 in).
Museum of Fine
Arts, Boston. This
is a variation of
the pastoral genre,
executed with the
new Impressionist
plein-air technique,
and without any
hidden meanings.

96

♦ *Above:* Dahlias,
c. 1873.
Oil on canvas,
73 × 54 cm
(28 3/4 × 21 1/4 in).
Musée d'Orsay,
Paris.

♦ *Opposite:* Small
Delft Vase with
Bouquet, *c. 1874.*
Oil on canvas,
41 × 27 cm
(16 1/8 × 10 5/8 in).
Musée d'Orsay,
Paris.

♦ *Above:* Flowers
in a Vase, *1873-75.*
Oil on canvas,
56 × 46 cm
(22 × 18 1/8 in).
Hermitage Museum,
St. Petersburg.

♦ *Opposite above:*
Still Life with Jug
and Cup, *1873-77.*
Oil on canvas,
20.5 × 18.5 cm
(8 × 7 1/4 in).
Bridgestone Museum
of Art, Tokyo.

♦ *Opposite below:*
The Sideboard,
1873-77.
Oil on canvas,
65 × 81 cm
(25 1/2 × 31 7/8 in).
Szépmüvészeti
Museum, Budapest.
The élan vital *of the*
individual objects
in this composition,
which are in such
vivid contrast to the

black barrier of the
sideboard, reveals
how Cézanne,
especially in his still
lifes, refused to adopt
the dissolution
so typical of
Impressionism:
rather than
rendering the motif,
he was determined to
dominate it and lend
it structure and form.

♦ Opposite: Self-portrait with a Beret, c. 1873-75. Oil on canvas, 55 × 38 cm (21 5/8 × 15 in). Hermitage Museum, St. Petersburg.

The bold brushwork, dabs of colour and contorted surface areas lend forceful expression to the artist's intense face.

♦ Above: Madame Cézanne Leaning on a Table, 1873-77. Oil on canvas, 61 × 50 cm (24 × 19 5/8 in). Private Collection, Geneva.

102

♦ *Above:* The
Temptation of St.
Anthony, *1873-77.*
Oil on canvas,
47 × 56 cm
(18 1/2 × 22 in).
Musée d'Orsay,
Paris. In returning
to this motif,
Cézanne sets the
figure of the
temptress in the
middle of the
composition, the
saint at left together
with the devil and,
at right, the groups
of putti and the trees.
The literary source
was probably the
Queen of Sheba in
Flaubert's Temptation
of St. Anthony *(1847).*

♦ *Right:* Le déjeuner
sur l'herbe, *c. 1875.*
Oil on canvas,
21 × 27.5 cm
(8 1/4 × 10 7/8 in).
Musée de l'Orangerie,
Paris. Up until
around 1880
Cézanne painted
many variations of
groups of figures in
idyllic settings in
which he did away
with nudity and
eroticism and
introduced random
activities. In this
canvas a man,
accompanied by
a child, carries
a basket of apples
(with their
connotation of the

fruit of temptation)
and another man is
obviously not part
of the group (is this
Cézanne himself?).
The canvases
of Giorgione and
Manet were always
a conscious or
unconscious element
in these scenes, and
many of the figures
reappear in
Cézanne's paintings
of bathers.

104

♦ Bathers, 1874-75.
Oil on canvas,
38 × 46 cm
(15 × 18 1/8 in).
Metropolitan
Museum of Art,
New York.
Trees are never
a purely decorative
component for
Cézanne; they have
an essential, almost
human role in his
natural settings.
In his first canvases
of bathers they are
often focal points of
the scene, taking on
a symbolic meaning
vis-à-vis the human
figures. Five female
nudes are on the
banks of a river and
the one in the water
is going to the other
side, where an
illuminated area is
dominated by a tree
in the form of a
cross. The nudes and
white drapery at left
are both enigmatic
and universal; the
tree, which in other
contexts evokes the
Garden of Eden, here
becomes a symbol
of redemption.

♦ Five Male Bathers,
1875-77.
Oil on canvas,
24 × 25 cm
(9 7/16 × 9 7/8 in).
Musée d'Orsay,
Paris.
These powerful,
statuesque, mute
nudes are no longer
set in the pyramidal
composition of his
early bathers,
and the landscape
has more open
space. The gestures
and poses hark back
to purification rites
found in ancient
sculpture and
the drawings of
the old masters,
and are a prelude
to the bathers
executed from 1890
to 1900.

♦ *Above:* Provençal Landscape, *c. 1875. Watercolour, 37.5 × 49.5 cm (14 3/4 × 19 1/2 in). Kunsthaus, Zurich.*

♦ *Opposite above:* Three Bathers, *c. 1875-77. Pencil, watercolour and gouache, 11.4 × 12.7 cm (4 1/2 × 5 in). National Museum of Wales, Cardiff.*

♦ *Opposite below:* Three Female Bathers, *1875-77. Oil on canvas, 19 × 22 cm (7 1/2 × 8 5/8 in). Musée d'Orsay, Paris. Roger Fry says that Cézanne seems to have a predilection for representing unattractive women and attributes this to his emotional reaction to sex and sexual inhibition. With the female bathers he almost* always adopts a pyramidal or triangular construction of the figures, which are often derived from baptism scenes in the art of the past, and the series of three female bathers is no exception to this. In executing these canvases, he draws from personal memories as well as from visual and literary images in the works of others.

108

♦ The Road (The
Wall), *1875-76.*
Oil on canvas,
49.8 × 65 cm
(19 5/8 × 25 5/8 in).
Private Collection,
USA.
This landscape
is illuminated by
a warm sun and
revolves around the
houses with their red
roofs and the wall
filled with light,
dominated and
framed by a group
of trees the leaves

of which seem
weightless, like a
flight of golden spots
in the sky. In the
background is
Sainte-Victoire, a
sort of anticipation
of the canvases of
the following years
in which the artist
reveals his greatness
by transcending all
details in order
to render nature
in the all-embracing
unity of a vibrant,
timeless light.

♦ Study for "The Flayed Man," c. 1875-76. Pencil, 22 × 12 cm (8 5/8 × 4 3/4 in). Art Institute, Chicago. Cézanne's passion for drawing human figures began at the Académie Suisse. Much later in his career he executed drawings copied from statues and great paintings in the Louvre.

110

♦ *Opposite:* Self-portrait in a White Turban, *1875-77.* *Oil on canvas,* *55.5 × 46 cm* *(21 7/8 × 10 5/8 in).* *Neue Pinakothek,* *Munich. Year after* *year, Cézanne* studied and painted *his face objectively,* *choosing unusual* *kinds of head-dresses* *and emphasizing* *his anti-social* *attitude by looking* *directly at the* *spectator.*

♦ *Above:* Madame Cézanne in a Red Armchair, *1877. Oil* *on canvas, 72.4 × 56* *cm (28 1/2 × 22 in).* *Museum of Fine* *Arts, Boston.* *Hortense was an* *extremely patient* model for Cézanne, *and his many* *portraits of her* *betray his increasing* *need for structural* *order and his desire* *to create solid and* *powerful forms. Here* *he is interested* mostly in the *changing nature* *of the colours, the* *intensity of which* *permeates her face* *and clothes, the chair* *and the background,* *creating a strange* *unity of the planes.*

112

♦ *Above:* Victor Chocquet, *1877.* *Oil on canvas,* *35 × 27 cm* *(13 3/4 × 10 5/8 in).* *P. Mellon Collection,* *Upperville, Virginia.*

Cézanne idealizes the elongated face of this customs official who became the friend and patron of the Impressionist painters.

♦ *Opposite:* Portrait of Victor Chocquet, *1876-77.* *Oil on canvas,* *45.7 × 36.8 cm* *(16 × 14 1/2 in).* *Private Collection.*

The bold colour reveals the artist's vigorous, agitated brushwork that applies thick layers of paint rich in vibrations and hues.

114

115

♦ *Opposite above:*
The Eternal
Feminine, *c. 1877.*
Oil on canvas,
43 × 53 cm
(17 × 20 7/8 in).
Private Collection,
New York. The men

gathered around the
female idol may
represent the vices
and hypocrisy of
bourgeois society,
but the more one
analyzes this canvas,
the stranger it seems.

♦ *Opposite below:*
The Eternal
Feminine, *c. 1877.*
Watercolour,
17.5 × 23 cm
(6 7/8 × 9 in).
Private Collection,
Zurich.

♦ *Above:* Olympia,
c. 1877. Watercolour,
24 × 26 cm
(9 7/16 × 10 1/4 in).
Museum of Art,
Philadelphia.

116

♦ Roofs, 1877.
Oil on canvas,
47 × 59 cm
(8 1/2 × 23 1/4 in).
Hahnloser Collection,
Bern.
In rendering the
sensory world,
Cézanne, fresh from
his Impressionist
experience, paints
outdoors, 'on the
motif.' In his quest
for structural order
he attaches equal
importance to every
element of the
pictorial
composition and
tends to distinguish
them through
simplification.

♦ Still Life, c. 1877.
Oil on canvas,
60.6 × 73.6 cm
(23 7/8 × 29 in).
Metropolitan
Museum of Art,
New York.
According to the
critic Rivière, the
backdrop of olive-
yellow wallpaper
with blue flowers
makes it possible to
date this work, since
the wallpaper was
in a house the artist
inhabited in 1877.
Cézanne's handling
of light serves
to render the
consistency of the
forms rather than
dissolve them. Echoes
of Manet can be
noted in the white
drapery.

118

♦ *Left:* Still Life with Soup Tureen, *c. 1877. Oil on canvas, 65 × 81.5 cm (25 5/8 × 32 in). Musée d'Orsay, Paris. "His beautiful still lifes," writes Georges Rivière, "so exact in the relationship of tones, have a solemn quality of truth. In all his paintings the artist produces emotion because he himself experiences, in the face of nature, a violent emotion that his craftsmanship transmits to the canvas." This still life, which was probably painted at Pontoise in 1877, captures the play of light subtly reflected on the humble objects. There is hardly any shadow. On the wall, which extends the composition, are three canvases, one of which is a landscape by Pissarro.*

♦ *Above:* Still Life with Open Drawer, *1877-79. Oil on canvas, 33 × 41 cm (13 × 16 1/8 in). Private Collection, Switzerland. The objects are a pretext for a perfectly self-contained pictorial construction, a harmoniously woven fabric with a life of its own.*

120

♦ The Seine at Bercy (after Guillaumin), 1876-78. Oil on canvas, 59 × 72 cm (23 1/4 × 28 3/8 in). Kunsthalle, Hamburg. Pissarro's influence led Cézanne to refine his palette and composition, and also served to stimulate his interest in structural order. From this period onwards, the artist's representations of reality were increasingly synthetic and balanced.

♦ Apples and Pears, *their radical,*
c. 1877-79. *shifting viewpoints,*
Oil on canvas, *Cézanne is able to*
26 × 33 cm *make everyday*
(10 1/4 × 13 in). *objects monumental*
Museum of Art, *and epic, lending*
Philadelphia. *them a sense of*
In these simplified *timelessness and*
compositions with *permanence.*

122

♦ *Above:* Bather with Arms Spread, *1877-78.* *Oil on canvas,* *33 × 24 cm* *(13 × 9 7/16 in).* *Private Collection,* *Zurich. This is the first in a series of isolated bathers – upright, contemplative, self-absorbed.*

♦ *Opposite:* Self-portrait, *1877-80.* *Oil on canvas,* *25.2 × 14.5 cm* *(10 × 5 3/4 in).* *Musée d'Orsay,* *Paris.* *The face, with its intense glance and thick beard hiding the mouth, was painted in a detached, meditctive spirit.*

The Structural Use
of Colour

"As the many studies to which I have dedicated myself have given me only negative results, and as I am afraid of only too justified criticism, I had resolved to work in silence until the day when I should feel myself able to defend theoretically the result of my attempts," Cézanne wrote to Octave Maus on 25 November 1889.

After the third Impressionist exhibition he moved farther and farther away from the formal vocabulary that had allowed him to discover the luminosity of colour and returned to his secluded meditation on nature; he pared down forms to their essentials, highlighting the structural framework of the image. Although he continued to paint *en plein air*, he was determined to attain a more solid and consistent organization of the sensory world, which could be achieved only by surpassing the Impressionist approach, its search for spontaneity.

Profound and direct observation of reality, which allowed him to perceive the essence of things, became the indispensable condition of his painting.

He limited his choice of motifs – the bay at L'Estaque, the houses nestled on the hill at Gardanne, Jas de Bouffan, Sainte-Victoire – and painted them from different viewpoints. The recording of sensations was slow and painstaking, both in the physical and psychological sense. Space expanded and contracted; the distance seen with the mind's eye was ambiguously merged with nearby elements. Traditional perspective was cancelled, the surface space was filled with palpitating flattened planes and all the points in space were connected in a continuous network. Cézanne does not impose formulas on nature. Every brushstroke seems to be at once the fruit of on-site perception and the search for the subsequent organization of this sensory experience. As Renato Barilli says, he effects a retinal correction of pure vision, he adapts the brushstroke to the surface context, and the colour unveils meanings that transcend mere appearance.

L'Estaque (1876) is the prototype of a series of views from above that he executed in the following years. The elevated horizon line, the foreground that seems to be overturned towards the surface of the canvas, the compressed space and reduced perspective – show that the inner structure of Cézanne's works is now just as much the result of choice as of his response to nature. In *The Château at Médan* (1879-81) the diagonal brushstrokes model the foliage of the trees, the clouds and parts of the buildings, while the space is flattened and the distances are shortened, thus reducing the sensation of depth. *The Bridge at Maincy* (1879-80) is a beautiful and exemplary work. Having eliminated the patches of colour Pissarro usually adopted, Cézanne makes use of large colour areas that are woven into an indivisible whole. The structure is solid and every brushstroke corresponds to another one to create a tautly organized, clear-cut symmetry. "Everything we see is dispersed, disappears. Nature is always the same, but nothing that appears before our eyes remains. Art must offer the thrill of her perpetuity. We must represent her as eternal." Cézanne concentrated on the 'philosophical' rather than the merely topographical aspects of nature; he painted an old bridge reflected in the river, a dark and silent forest, still waters, tangled vegetation. Thick, varied brushstrokes were linked in a rhythmical and chromatic unity; nature and space consisted of colour. "Drawing and outline are not distinct. By the very fact of painting, one draws," Cézanne declared. The more colour harmonizes, the more precise is the drawing and the more it is able to create a coherent structure. He used local colour, but to create depth; it did not capture the fleeting impressions of light (and here lies his departure from Impressionist procedure), but rather the inner life of the subject: light was no longer an atmospheric accident but an intrinsic part of the whole. The need to render the complexity of the plant world – albeit through a process of reduction and synthesis – induced Cézanne to immerse himself into it and let the tree trunks play an important role in establishing the verticality of the composition, while the diagonal lines suggest depth, create a strongly knit architectural structure and extend the bounds of the canvas surface.

In the landscapes of L'Estaque we see that he has amplified the process of solidifying nature. The sea is never a fluid mass; in order to reduce the depth, Cézanne has it extend almost like a flat, vertical plane over the surface; it is not ruffled by the wind and its waves have only faint traces of white; its liquid quality is virtually non-existent. An Impressionist artist would have represented its constant flux, while Cézanne feels that even the sea has a right to its own plastic qualities. It is always seen from above, often under an overhead sun, with a pictorial procedure that ignores the breakdown of colour in light and concentrates rather on rendering the material properties of painting. Cézanne preferred the midday sun, when the blue of the Mediterranean sky was saturated and everything was tinged with the most intense hues: ochre, brick red, cobalt blue, emerald green. But he depicted the changing phenomena of nature in a suspended state that permitted him to grasp their eternal quality. In the various versions of *Gulf of Marseilles Seen from L'Estaque*, the composition, divided into three parts, is arranged in a precise order: in the foreground, the wooded hills or houses, then the sea, and lastly the mountains, over which the sky delimits the canvas. The colour values are of equal strength, the different elements are no longer isolated but are unified by the structural function of colour.

In the views of Sainte-Victoire – at times represented in monumental fashion, placed on broad-ranging horizontal lines with the elements of the landscape arranged in parallel areas to create an effect of compact grandiosity; at other times set at the end of a wide valley animated by houses, fields, roads, trees and bridges – Cézanne kept the various components of the landscape under tight control, establishing a continuity of the painterly qualities that eliminates all possible dispersion. When necessary, he introduced the stark verticality of a tree isolated in the middle, balanced by a group of trees at the side, in order to create a sort of setting for the image. Or he would frame the panorama with the leaves of a large pine, a fundamental cohesive element in space, the branches following the outline of the mountain.

These works call to mind Hokusai's *One Hundred Views of Mt. Fuji*, which were first seen in Paris in 1883; the Japanese artist's cycle of woodcuts is a tribute to the Sacred Mountain, a sign of yearning for artistic perfection and immortality. Cézanne's relationship to Sainte-Victoire was perhaps analogous to this.

When the mountain appears amidst the bare branches of the *Chestnut Trees at the Jas de Bouffan in Winter*, it is no longer a mirage in a world dominated by crystalline organic forms; but when its southern slope is seen from Gardanne, it is again in the guise of a gigantic rampart, an indestructible work of nature that will survive the ephemeral and transient. Already in 1870 Sainte-Victoire was an important compositional element in *The Railway Cutting*, and in the following decades it took on ever growing importance, in the end becoming central to the overall structure.

With their solemn, intricate composition and cadenced equilibrium between masses and space, Cézanne's still lifes – which according to Rivière have classical features – reveal the artist's empathy with the silent inner life of objects, his desire to create an order that would slowly give rise to a radically new image of the world. The preference for spherical forms, the ever more intense endeavour to define volumes, the architectural construction of the composition, the attention paid to the effect of light, the use of multiple viewpoints to establish space and perspective – are all aspects of still life that he strove to perfect for a long time. Conceived in an empty space, the forms reveal, in the very density of the inanimate objects, that Cézanne sought to integrate signs of continuous tension and conflict into an organic order. From within an apparent symmetry and balance the different elements are in dialectical opposition to one another: an inevitable and dramatic rejection of traditional pictorial organization. This upheaval forces space and volume to conform to the artist's vision. "I want to astonish Paris with an apple," Cézanne stated. He began painting apples in his Impressionist period, and they soon became one of his favourite motifs: an obsession with erotic overtones, a rotundity that was not totally innocent. He painted slowly and therefore chose the apple because it is the fruit that retains its qualities the longest; furthermore, with its form this fruit casts its colour reflections on nearby objects and in turn reflects their colours. Cézanne's conception of form is organic-dynamic: the apple is a body in expansion; he paints it from the edge towards the middle, from the furthest to the nearest point.

Since the still life implies a 'close-up' of the objects, physical proximity to them, it allows the artist to perceive their volume and mass. Whereas the Impressionists asserted that air is necessarily present in a painting, in Cézanne's still lifes the air between the painter and the objects painted is virtually non-existent, and the objects reveal their volume to the observer.

The background is blocked, both when the artist establishes a viewpoint from above and when he avoids depth by means of some obstacle and concentrates on the play of volumes and colours. With time the outlines of the fruit become more and more evident, the individual parts of the composition are highlighted and the wide-ranging play of values instils life into them. New, bold compositional configurations come into being.

At first the surface is schematically divided into two parts – the horizontal plane that acts as a support is darker, and the background is lighter; the objects retain their volumetric unity by means of colour contrasts. Sometimes the canvas is divided more elaborately into horizontal, vertical and oblique lines. Through the organization into closed angles, the natural elements in the canvas become life-enhancing. But the planes can also fan out before the spectator's gaze, giving rise to a sort of panorama that merges the different viewpoints, eliminates the obstacles, dispenses with all rules of perspective, and

creates an impressive symphony of tangible material qualities. Flowers can also 'defy' their architectural framework. *The Blue Vase* (1883-87) is noteworthy for its gamut of light, intense and luminous colours that saturate the entire surface. Careful and refined tonal modulation works hand in hand with the richness of the colours. This is a lyrical work totally liberated from spatial constrictions and moves towards the bursting vitality of animate, rather than inanimate, objects. If landscape needs solidity in order to take on life in painting, for the same reason flowers sometimes need to lighten the weight of the material properties of painting. The composition is carefully calculated, the vase is placed centrally in a play of vertical lines with the objects around it; but the flowers reaching out in different directions defy any schematic configuration. This is confirmed by the oblique line behind the vase which fades away near the edge of the latter. The severe construction of the canvas is attenuated by such 'irregularities' and certain textural areas seem to contradict the very substance of the objects, thus revealing the artist's creative struggle.

The influence of Impressionism is still strongly felt in Cézanne's oeuvre. His gradual mastery of the colour blue – based on the pictorial values of distance and depth that derive from Poussin, from Goethe's theory of colours and Nietzsche's definition of Wagner's *Lohengrin* as "blue music" – served to enhance objects and to achieve balance among the other chromatic values. The colour blue enables the artist to flatten space without making it seem restricted or crushed; it animates space inwardly with ethereal vibrations.

The 1877 *Portrait of Victor Chocquet* is executed with thick layers of paint and seems to be structured without lines or planes, whereas Cézanne's command of spatial configuration is really firm. He did many portraits of his art collector friend – standing, full-length and seated – with a play of vertical and horizontal lines and succeeded in capturing Chocquet's sensitivity and humanity. The portraits

of his wife Hortense are impassive; the model is depicted in a detached, abstract manner. Far removed from the vital, sanguine fascination of Impressionist images, Hortense seems to be a symbol of Cézanne's inability to communicate. Her head is in the shape of an egg, a perfect abstract form; her face is expressionless and the artist's interest in volumes sometimes reaches its peak here – a masterful way of rendering absence. It has been said that Cézanne painted his friends and the members of his family as if they were apples. Yet his portraits bear witness to his desire not to exclude humans from his world, even though the prerogatives of painting sometimes eclipse the human factor. In *Portrait of Louis Guillaume* the head and body of the boy are elementary and motionless; the stolid face, which perhaps reflects the model's introverted character, is accentuated by the gamut of low-key tonalities and the depth of the dark hues.

The self-portraits – he executed over thirty of them – represent another chapter in his artistic production. They reveal his introspective gifts and continuous self-examination. His direct gaze, with his protuberant forehead and large head sometimes covered with a hat or beret, indicate his intention to offer himself to a potential interlocutor. The most formidable work of this genre is *Self-portrait with Palette* (1885-87), a large canvas in which Cézanne depicts himself in the act of painting, the only self-portrait in which he is not looking at the spectator. A solid figure is 'invaded' by painting as if the material of the palette has saturated the entire canvas, as if the canvas he is working on in the self-portrait, and the wall behind him, were illuminating him with multicoloured light. He painted this work as a mirror image, with the palette in his right hand as if he were left-handed. The subject and surrounding space merge. The brushwork is delicate, with layers of paint applied lightly and traces of white that indicate an unfinished quality: an incompleteness that always assailed Cézanne and that was proof of his vitality.

An important part of his production

were his nudes, which are connected to the paintings and emotions of his youth. The female nudes are particularly disturbing; unattractive, stout, with large backs, protruding spines and merely rough-hewn faces. The 'anti-graceful' nudes in *Five Female Bathers*, absolutely lacking in erotic fascination, remind one of *The Eternal Feminine*. Their masculine faces that seem to be carved out of stone discourage any psychological involvement and invite comparison with Picasso's *Demoiselles d'Avignon* (painted twenty-five years later), and the rotation of their bodies and multiple viewpoints anticipate certain aspects of Cubism and Futurism. But even for our late 20th-century eyes this canvas is startling. According to Marie-Louise Krumrine, these bathers represent a fusion of Christian and pagan elements and allude to the fountain of youth and baptism, the renewal of the flesh and the spirit. The body-soul dualism was already present in Cézanne's *Déjeuner sur l'herbe* and *Pastoral*, though it must be said that his bathers are more mysterious figures. On the one hand the nudes seem to be part of a pagan rite celebrating physical energy, and on the other they can be taken as Christian motifs (the Garden of Eden, temptation, purification through baptism). But above all, they represent Cézanne's determination to create a modern image that would boldly rejuvenate the worn-out classical models (always lurking in the background in any representation of a nude), to the point of eliminating conventional beauty.

The Great Male Bather (1885), an isolated monumental figure, has been interpreted by Meyer Schapiro as a probable indication of the artist's solitude, which are mirrored in the features of the sky and earth – the former airy and the latter solid. This canvas is an allusion to the conflict between passion and contemplation, active life and isolation. In the end the meditative aspect triumphs, but the body retains its warm and powerful colour, while the outside world – an all-enveloping void – is cold and distant. This is a statue whose monumentality is enhanced in the landscape.

126

♦ Above: Self-portrait, 1878-80. Oil on canvas, 60 × 46 cm (23 5/8 × 18 1/8 in). The Phillips Collection, Washington, DC.

♦ Opposite: Self-portrait, c. 1878. Oil on canvas, 66 × 55 cm (26 × 21 5/8 in). Private Collection. The German poet Rilke made the following comment on this work: "It is drawn with absolute surety, harsh but rounded, the forehead consisting of a single block the solidity of which persists even where it dissolves into forms and planes and becomes the demarcation of a thousand outlines; this is where the face begins, preceded by the bearded chin which is rendered with incredible intensity, stroke by stroke."

♦ *Above:* Allegorical Figure of a River, Study after Delacroix, *c. 1878-81. Pencil, 12 × 21 cm (4 3/4 × 8 1/4 in). Art Institute, Chicago.*

♦ *Right:* The Gulf of Marseilles Seen from L'Estaque, *1878-79. Oil on canvas, 58 × 72 cm (22 7/8 × 28 3/8 in). Musée d'Orsay, Paris.*

The composition is divided into distinct areas characterized by different colours and brushwork. The horizon line is high and Cézanne has eliminated *classical perspective by superimposing planes that rise as they move away from the spectator.*

130

♦ The Bridge at Maincy, *1879-80. Oil on canvas, 58.5 × 72.5 cm (23 × 28 1/2 in). Musée d'Orsay, Paris. Here Cézanne pinpoints a patch* of landscape and *defines a solidly constructed motif. The bridge is a simple geometric form, a rectangle lying motionless over the river that extends* from one end of the *canvas to the other. Water, bridge, trees – everything is organized into a structure of vertical, horizontal, diagonal and circular lines,* as if the artist had *discovered the urge to depict the solidity of the sensory world by 'freezing' the open space of Impressionist painting.*

131

♦ Farmyard at
Auvers, 1879-80.
Oil on canvas,
63 × 52 cm
(24 7/8 × 20 7/16 in).
Musée d'Orsay,
Paris.
The red roofs and
ochre walls of the
farmhouse, with
their dark outline,
stand out clearly
against the blue sky.
The corners and
other geometric
forms lend
consistency to the
buildings in the
midst of nature's
pulsating disorder.

132

♦ Five Male Bathers, 1879-80. Oil on canvas, 35 × 39 cm (13 3/4 × 15 3/8 in). Institute of Arts, Detroit. Drawing inspiration from Giorgione, Titian, Rubens and Poussin, Cézanne integrates the human figure into the landscape in order to define the relationship between man and nature. This work may hark back to his childhood at Aix when he and his friends swam in the Arc River, or it may depict soldiers bathing in the river.

♦ Auvers Seen from the Val Harmé, 1879-82. Oil on canvas, 73 × 92 cm (28 3/4 × 36 1/4 in). Private Collection, Zurich. Although he had decided to live in Provence, Cézanne returned periodically to Paris and Île de France, where he filtered his Impressionist experience by means of his uniform, parallel brushstrokes, which lent solidity to the landscape. Impressionist space expands due to the light and is lightened by the circulation of air, becoming almost limitless. Cézanne was obsessed by the 'motif' and sought a well-structured, logically ordered subject in the landscape.

134

♦ Melting Snow
at Fontainebleau,
1879-82.
*Oil on canvas,
73 × 102 cm
(28 3/4 × 40 1/8 in).
Museum of Modern
Art, New York.
The Fontainebleau
forest, the favourite
site for the Barbizon
school and young
Impressionist
painters, was also a
source of inspiration
for Cézanne up to
his old age. There is
something absolute,
almost religious,*
*about his
relationship with
trees; he loved their
verticality, the way
they resisted the
rhythm of the
changing seasons,
their function as
a sort of filter
of spatial depth
and as structural
elements. The cold,
clear light, the bluish
shadows, and the
granular sky are
symbols of both his
identification with
nature and its
sublimation.*

♦ The Château
at Médan, 1879-81.
Oil on canvas,
59 × 72 cm
(23 1/4 × 28 3/8 in).
Art Gallery and
Museum, Glasgow.
Zola's luxurious
house, which he
purchased in 1878,
was the subject of
several of Cézanne's
paintings. This
work, which once
belonged to Gauguin,
reveals the artist's
obstinate struggle
to attain a new
equilibrium of forms
and colours, a new
spatial density, by
means of brushwork
employed to highlight
the consistency
of objects.
The frontality of
this work is offset
by the luminous
colours. "Reading
nature," Cézanne
said, "means being
able to see it in
the guise of an
interpretation
of harmoniously
grouped dabs
of colour... Painting
means recording
one's coloured
sensations."

136

♦ Still Life with Receptacles, Fruit and Cloth, *1879-82. Oil on canvas, 45 × 57 cm (17 5/8 × 22 3/4 in). Hermitage Museum, St. Petersburg. Cézanne's still lifes were acquiring more and more inner* cohesion and stylization. Over and above their erotic overtones, apples are key elements in the artist's lifelong struggle; they reminded him of his first meeting with Zola, when the future writer gave him some apples after he had defended Zola from some bullies. Cézanne later said he wanted to astonish Paris with an apple – a common object, to be sure, but the motif par excellence for him. According to the critic Meyer Schapiro, the breadth and surety of the canvases in which drapery and fruit are arranged in a complicated but balanced manner, demonstrate that for Cézanne the apple was as important as the human body.

♦ Still Life with Jar,
Fruit, Tablecloth
and Glass, *1879-82.
Oil on canvas,
66 × 73 cm
(23 5/8 × 28 3/4 in).
Musée de l'Orangerie,
Paris. The diagonally
placed knife that
divides the space is a
tribute to Manet.*

*The forms are
simplified and take
on a volumetric
solidity that is
coupled with intense
colouring, as if the
colours themselves
modelled the objects,
while the different
planes highlight the
overall structure.*

138

♦ *Above:* Self-Portrait with Olive Wallpaper, *1880-81.* *Oil on canvas, 34 × 27 cm (13 3/8 × 10 5/8 in). National Gallery, London.* *The angular shapes in the background contrast with the massive rotundity* *of the artist's head and shoulders. This combination of organic and geometric elements shows that the wallpaper was chosen as an integral part of highly concentrated pictorial handling.*

♦ *Opposite:* Self-portrait, *1879-82.* *Oil on canvas, 65 × 51 cm (25 5/8 × 20 1/8 in). Kunstmuseum, Bern.* *The critic Louis Vauxelles gave the following description of Cézanne in 1904: "Paul Cézanne is a legendary figure,* *with a coarse, bristly face, his body wrapped in a carter's rough woollen cloak. But this Cézanne is a master."*

140

♦ *Above*: Bather,
*1879-1906. Pencil
and watercolour,
22.2 × 17.4 cm
(8 3/4 × 6 7/8 in).
Wadsworth
Atheneum, Hartford.*

♦ *Opposite above:*
The Artist's Son,
*1877-79.
Oil on canvas,
17 × 15 cm
(6 5/8 × 6 in).
Metropolitan
Museum of Art,*

*New York.
Cézanne's portrait of
his son is not at all
sentimental nor is it
a character study;
he is interested only
in structuring the
composition.*

♦ *Opposite below:*
The Artist's Son,
*1880-85.
Oil on canvas,
35 × 38 cm
(13 3/4 × 15 in).
Musée de l'Orangerie,
Paris.*

144

♦ Mont Sainte-
Victoire, *1882-85.*
Oil on canvas,
60 × 73 cm
(23 5/8 × 28 3/4 in).
Pushkin Museum,
Moscow. "The very
aridity of the subject
gives Cézanne the
chance to create this
simplification and
regularization that
leads to
monumentality,"
states Lionello
Venturi, referring
to Sainte-Victoire
as an expression
of the artist's
structural ideal.

♦ *Above:* L'Estaque,
1882-81.
Oil on canvas,
59.7 × 73 cm
(23 1/2 × 28 3/4 in).
Musée d'Orsay,
Paris. Cézanne's
mother had a house
at L'Estaque, west
of Marseilles, where
the artist took refuge
during the Franco-
Prussian War. He
returned a few years
later and, attracted
by the
Mediterranean,
executed the few
seascapes in his
oeuvre.

♦ *Below:* L'Estaque
Seen through the
Pines, 1882-83.
Oil on canvas,
72.5 × 90 cm
(28 1/2 × 35 7/16 in).
Readers' Digest
Collection,
Pleasantville,
New York.

146

♦ *Opposite:*
L'Estaque, *c. 1882-85.*
Oil on canvas,
71.1 × 57.7 cm
(28 × 22 3/4 in).
Private Collection.
L. Guerry compares
the L'Estaque
canvases with those
of true 'primitive'
painters and
observes that the
difference between
the two types of
primitive handling
is that in Cézanne
the illusion of
perspective stems
from the fact that the
real (the airy
'container' and the
solid 'contents') is
treated like a unitary
plastic mass. It is
precisely because
the entire landscape
functions as a single
volume that the
profile of this volume
suggests the
existence of a third
dimension."

♦ *Above:* Rocky
Landscape, *1882-85.*
Oil on canvas,
73 × 91 cm
(28 3/4 × 35 7/8 in).
Museu de Arte,
São Paulo.
We seem to be looking
at the consequences
of a cataclysmic
volcanic eruption.
The rocky, barren
hills of Provence are
rendered with
grandiose harshness.
When Cézanne said
he could not paint
a landscape without
first having
experienced it, he
was referring to the
sensory acuteness
on which he based
his conception
of a visionary
composition.
Here the rock
expands and
contracts; the flat
slice of sea and thin
strip of sky take up
very little space.

148

♦ L'Estaque and the
Gulf of Marseilles,
1882-85.
Oil on canvas,
65 × 81 cm
(25 5/8 × 31 7/8 in).
Museum of Art,
Philadelphia.
From the early 1880s
on, the theme of the
Gulf of Marseilles
seen from L'Estaque
was the object of
pictorial handling
which makes sensory
data abstract
by using the body
of water and
mountains to create
spatial depth.
Cézanne helped later
generations of artists
discover Midi light;
Braque and Dufy
painted their most
Cézanne-like works
precisely at
L'Estaque.

♦ The Gulf of Marseilles Seen from L'Estaque, 1883-85. Oil on canvas, 73 × 100.4 cm (28 3/4 × 39 1/2 in). Metropolitan Museum of Art, New York. This landscape is viewed from above, the horizon line has been raised and the foreground flattened, the houses superimposed on the surface of the canvas, thus compressing the space. The perspective towards the horizon is reduced, so that what is distant is close to our glance, whereas what is near is rendered with few details, as if it were at the same distance. Cézanne's world is more stable and full of objects than the Impressionist world; the inclination of the vertical objects is a compelling way of involving us in his struggle for balance. Nothing is left to chance. Liberated from Impressionist procedure, the artist pursues more complex ideas, reduces his palette and concentrates on plastic ends and means.

150

♦ *Above:* Still Life with Cherries, Peaches, Vase and Tablecloth, *1883-87.* *Oil on canvas,* *50 × 61 cm* *(19 5/8 × 24 in).* *County Museum* *of Art, Los Angeles.*

♦ *Opposite:* The Blue Vase, *1883-87.* *Oil on canvas,* *61 × 50 cm* *(24 × 19 5/8 in).* *Musée d'Orsay,* *Paris. This sober,* *refined still life with* *luminous colours*

is dominated by a *subtle modulation of* *tonalities. The play* *of lines and balanced* *volumes create the* *space; the overall* *harmony is achieved* *through the use of* *varied hues of blue.*

152

♦ Still Life with Pots of Flowers,
c. 1883-87.
Watercolour,
24 × 31 cm
(9 7/16 × 11 1/2 in).
Cabinet des Dessins,
Musée du Louvre,
Paris.
The line of pots on the shelf was probably inspired by the hothouse at the Jas de Bouffan. Unlike his still lifes with fruit, which are among Cézanne's most complicated, laboured and heroic achievements, the flower motifs retain an air of ease and spontaneity that links them with analogous Impressionist works of the 1860s. The lyrical movement is perfectly balanced with the overall monumental solidity of the composition; the charm of these live plants is part and parcel of their absolute nature.

♦ Green Jug,
c. 1885-87.
Watercolour, 22 × 25
cm (8 5/8 × 9 7/8 in).
Cabinet des Dessins,
Musée du Louvre,
Paris. Thanks to the artist's capacity
to render volume,
this humble object
stands out with its
impressive presence,
which is reiterated
in the dark shadow.

154

♦ Still Life on a Table, c. 1885. Oil on canvas, 71 × 90 cm (28 × 35 7/16 in). Neue Pinakothek, Munich. This canvas has an almost musical perfection about it. It is carefully constructed, rich in motifs and at the same time without any central motif; it is surprisingly rich in decorative detail, with many variations and relationships.

The dominating structural element is the contrast between dark and light and between the objects in the foreground and the chest of drawers. Cézanne's quest for solidity and compactness embraces the colours and the equilibrium of the curves and lines. The tablecloth is a complex integration of straight and curved lines, a fantastic, dynamic, dialectical element.

♦ Tall Trees at the
Jas de Bouffan,
c. 1885-87.
Oil on canvas,
65 × 81 cm
(25 5/8 × 31 7/8 in).
Courtauld Institute
Galleries, London.

Cézanne's solemn,
immobile trees,
especially in the
landscapes executed
in the late 1880s,
evoke the grandiose
and heroic 17th-
century landscapes.

156

♦ *Opposite above:*
Trees and Houses,
c. 1885-87.
Oil on canvas,
68 × 92 cm
(26 3/4 × 36 1/4 in).
Metropolitan
Museum of Art,
New York.

♦ *Opposite below:*
Trees and Houses,
c. 1885-87.
Oil on canvas,
54 × 73 cm
(21 1/4 × 28 3/4 in).
Musée de l'Orangerie,
Paris.

♦ *Above:* Mont
Sainte-Victoire (The
Viaduct), *c. 1885-87.*
Oil on canvas,
65.4 × 81.5 cm
(25 3/4 × 32 1/8 in).
Metropolitan
Museum of Art,
New York.
The isolated tree
in the middle of the
canvas is a bold,
unorthodox element
that lends depth to
the landscape and
sets the foreground
in relief and links
it with the other
planes. Taking in the
entire breadth of the
broad valley,
Cézanne creates
an impression of
calm and plenitude.
The vertical-
horizontal contrast
is tempered by many
diagonal elements
in a series of
transitions that are
complemented
by the colour
modulations.

158

♦ Chestnut Trees
at the Jas de Bouffan
in Winter, *1885-87.*
Oil on canvas,
73 × 92 cm
(28 3/4 × 36 1/4 in).
Institute of Arts,
Minneapolis.
The artist has chosen
a viewpoint that
offers the least play
of perspective and
reduces the tension.
The mountain in
the distance is half-
hidden by the trees,
the trunks of which
are clear-cut organic
forms that are
immobile but not
rigid, while the
thin branches create
arabesques
in the sky.

♦ Chestnut Trees and Farmhouse at the Jas de Bouffan, *1885-87. Oil on canvas, 73 × 92 cm (28 3/4 × 36 1/4 in). Pushkin Museum, Moscow.*

This intense and solemn canvas reflects Cézanne's artistic maturity, his love for solitary nature captured in a moment of dazzling brilliance. Through a grandiose architectural structure, he translates his initial sensation of the real into a thoughtfully conceived composition.

160

♦ *Opposite:* The
Aqueduct, *1885-87.*
Oil on canvas,
92 × 74 cm
(36 1/4 × 29 1/8 in).
Pushkin Museum,
Moscow.

♦ *Above.* Mont Sainte-
Victoire. *1885-87.*
Oil on canvas,
67 × 92 cm
(26 3/8 × 36 1/4 in).
Courtauld Institute
Galleries, London.
The mountain
appears in all its
majesty, which is
underscored by the
large pine in the
foreground and
the broad valley.

Cézanne's creative
torment is expressed
in this geological
form, the peak
of which follows
the rhythmic
movement of the
branches above it.
The distant
landscape absorbs
the agitation of the
foreground.
Everything pulsates
with vitality in the

concert of changing
colours; a stable
world emerges from
a vast, incessant
movement. Yet the
canvas is permeated
by deep harmony
and is admirably
structured; an
example of this are
the branches which
accompany the
mountain slope
in the horizon.

162

♦ *Above:* Orchard,
c. 1885-87.
Oil on canvas,
61 × 50 cm
(24 × 19 5/8 in).
Academy of Fine
Arts, Honolulu.

♦ *Opposite:* Gardanne,
1885-86.
Oil on canvas,
81 × 65 cm
(31 7/8 × 25 5/8 in).
Metropolitan
Museum of Art,

New York.
The clusters of
houses in this hamlet
near Aix are
translated into a
landscape of pure,
geometric structures.

"The country here,
which has never
found a worthy
interpreter, harbours
many treasures,"
Cézanne wrote to
Chocquet in 1886.

164

♦ Madame Cézanne in Blue, *1885-87. Oil on canvas, 74 × 60 cm (29 1/8 × 23 5/8 in). Museum of Fine Arts, Houston. One of the many portraits of Hortense, with simplified volumes and summarily rendered facial features. The deep-set eyes, closed mouth, oval, elongated and impassive face, and parted hair – make up a sombre, mysterious image that is accentuated by a delicate palette.*

♦ Self-portrait with Palette, *1885-87. Oil on canvas, 92 × 73 cm (36 1/4 × 28 3/4 in). E.G. Bührle Foundation, Zurich. This monumental canvas has rare consistency.*

The palette seems to be an extension of the artist's body, and the slightly rectangular face and the hair reflect its outline. Palette, head, body and easel have an analogous solidity and objectivity that correspond to the ideal rectangle of the canvas – a flat, enclosed surface. The cold, austere colour is dominated by the blue-black of the jacket and the artist's beard and is animated by the vigorous contrasts in modelling that are clearly seen in the powerfully rendered jacket, the paints on the palette and the effects in the background.

♦ Opposite. The
Artist's Son, Paul,
1885-90.
Oil on canvas,
65.3 × 54 cm
(25 3/4 × 21 1/4 in).
National Gallery of
Art, Washington, DC.
Cézanne wrote his
last letter to his son
on 15 October 1906:
"I continue to work
with difficulty,
but in spite of this
something is
achieved... Since
sensations are the
basis of my work,
I think I am
impenetrable."

♦ Above: Five Female
Bathers, c. 1885-87.
Oil on canvas,
65.5 × 65.5 cm
(25 3/4 × 25 3/4 in).
Kunstmuseum,
Basle.
The heavy, grotesque
figures reflect the
artist's complex
relationship with
women. The source
and meaning of these
strange bathers is
not clear, but they
are certainly related.
Perhaps they evoke
a pagan baptism
ritual, though
certain Christian
elements can also
be recognized.
A comparison
between Cézanne's
Bathers and
Picasso's Demoiselles
d'Avignon
demonstrates that the
former's deformation
explodes with
excruciating
intensity and a
powerful sense
of mystery, without
Picasso's need
to resort to pictorial
expedients (which,
admittedly, are
revolutionary on
a formal level).

168

♦ The Gulf of
Marseilles Seen from
L'Estaque, *1886-90.*
Oil on canvas,
80 × 99.6 cm
(31 1/2 × 39 1/4 in).
Art Institute,
Chicago.
Seen from above, this
canvas presents a
vast space with well-
modelled, crystalline
elements. The houses,
water, hills and sky
are alternating areas
of movement and
repose. Devoid of
streets and humans,
this world is the
theme of a pure
vision, sun-filled
without gaiety, both
transient and
eternal. The strong
contrasts animate
the canvas and soft
colour modulations
and subtle
alignments unite
the different parts.
In this general state
of apparent
immobility nothing
is truly inert; the
dark water has a
breath of life, and the
sky contains delicate
vibrations.

♦ Mountains
in Provence,
1886-90.
Oil on canvas,
54 × 73 cm
(21 1/4 × 28 3/4 in).
National Museum
of Wales, Cardiff.
Cézanne views
nature as a solid
presence, something
we see but cannot
penetrate. This scene
offers a vast gamut
of sensations; from
the craggy,
dramatically
illuminated rocks
which are reddish in
the light and grey in
the shade, to the soft
slopes of the rounded
hills whose surface
is delicately rendered
in soft light. The
power and intense
harmony of this
canvas are achieved
by means of a
masterful mixture
of bold contrasts
and subtle harmony.

Everyday Objects Become Universal Symbols

In the second half of the 1880s Cézanne painted several landscapes with rivers and lakes, banks and bridges, in which he concentrated on rendering reflections, retaining their vibrant transparency while at the same time lending volumetric solidity to them. Later, these same motifs would be simplified and take on a crystalline form. The landscape acquired great compositional unity through a fluid modulation and fusion of colours. Cézanne painted motifs in his beloved Provence, seeking to discover the secrets of a land he never wanted to leave. He captured its simple, everyday facets, which were highly evocative for him: his family home, the farmhouses, the countryside where he roamed in his youth. These were fragments of a world in which the subjective and objective aspects of sense perception were blended.

In *House and Trees* (1892-94, Barnes Foundation), the building stands out in the landscape like a rudimental geometric object which is, however, scrutinized and penetrated so that it vibrates with life: everyday objects become universal symbols. The diagonal watercourse beside the wall, the crack in the exterior of the house, the irregular wall surrounding the house, the field glimpsed at the far right – are all enveloped in a clear, unifying light that avoids a clear-cut contrast between open and enclosed space. The linear forms of the trees, which serve to create spatial rhythm, impart a sense of distance yet merge with the countryside at certain points. From this time forward Cézanne on the one hand defined the plastic qualities of objects with increasing clarity, and on the other integrated the different elements into a unified whole that was emblematic of the complexity of the universe.

At times nature is grandiose and inscrutable; Cézanne tries to discover its secret structure by highlighting its immutable, timeless aspects. Scenes that are powerful while expressing great serenity, are based on strong contrasts, on the equilibrium between unstable, opposing forces. He creates images of a solitary world rich in

accidental, chaotic elements, vaguely organic forms absorbed by the vegetation. For example, *Rocks* (1894-98) is a dark, passionate canvas consisting of a convoluted, impenetrable plot of land filled with obstacles. The continuous undermining and re-establishment of perspective denotes strong feeling. 'The rocks ended up occupying the entire landscape... as chaotic as the mysterious, unfathomable ruins of a city of the distant past,' Flaubert says in his *Sentimental Education* in a dramatic description of the Fontainebleau forest, the site that most probably corresponds to the one in Cézanne's canvas.

In this same period his still lifes took on a monumental character; the volume of the objects depicted was conveyed by simplifying the outlines, while the arrangement of the elements became agitated, driven by an inner, centripetal driving force. A series of statements by Cézanne reveals that still lifes were much more important to him than mere compositional exercises. As he said to Gasquet: "What I have not yet managed to achieve, what I shall never manage in a figure or a portrait, I have perhaps approached here... in these still lifes." In these works Cézanne does much more than merely evoke inanimate objects; he paints them with loving intensity, sensuousness, ecstasy. "Objects influence each other completely... Imperceptibly they spread their influence, by means of their auras, as we do by means of looks and words." Starting off from his sensations, he threw himself totally into the patient observation of things and meditated on the fusion of planes, the mutual building up of colours, the harmonious relationships among the pictorial elements, pouring his love for the fullness of life into them. Small wonder that in 1892, Félix Fénéon, commenting on a Symbolist exhibition, said: "Three apples by Cézanne are able to strike and move one, they can even be mystical." *Kitchen Still Life* (1888-90) is proof of Cézanne's need to complicate the 'rules of the game' by elaborating more complex and dynamic groupings

among the various pictorial elements. Multiple viewpoints almost refute the unity of the composition; the unstable foreground close to the observer and the imbalance apparent in the upper left are counterpoised by the large basket that occupies the space between the table and the wall. Elements that by themselves are suspended, interact in mutual equilibrium. The cloth with its disorderly folds is antithetical to the rotundity of the fruit and receptacles and, curiously enough, is solid in order to lend shape to what is fluid. In *Still Life with Basket of Apples* (1890-94) as well, superimposed objects give the impression of an apparently casual construction, while it is really carefully thought out. The dissonance established among the details creates overall unity. A luminous, robust and clear colour is tempered in the larger elements and becomes more intense in the smaller ones.

There is also the originality of *Still Life with a Bottle of Peppermint Syrup* (1890-94), with its contracted space and the intricate, rigid folds of the cloth which is a veritable receptacle of objects that manifest their solidity, weight, and opacity or transparency. This is a magnificent canvas because of the inventiveness of its lines and movement, the richness and momentum of its curves (the blue cloth with its amazing play of rhythms). Cézanne employs multiple viewpoints so that the various elements have their own autonomous space in the overall arrangement. The objects, which touch one another and are tilted towards one another, represent his conflicts; they go beyond the limits of the mere recording of sensation and suggest fundamental problems of existence. The tangible sensuousness of the fruit and bottles is no less intense than in preceding still lifes, but here they play an increasingly important role in a more ambitious pictorial construction. It is as if we were witnessing the last act of a drama – a final burst of fine chromatic and compositional complexity.

Cézanne's rendering of the human figure confirms his growing solitude.

In the portraits of Hortense – magnificent examples of painting – there is no room for reality: the venue is that of art, in which the artist captures enduring qualities and values through immobility and inscrutability. The handling of the figure and space is cold and detached, the attenuation of the features serves to achieve compositional balance.

In *Madame Cézanne in a Yellow Chair* (1890-94) the elements that conflict with traditional perspective seem to anticipate, albeit allusively, the Cubist and Futurist ideographic handling of space. *Madame Cézanne in the Conservatory*, despite the scattered light touches, retains the usual compactness and inscrutability: the continuous border of the forehead, the oval face set in the concave area of the hair, the formal regularity of the nose, mouth and chin – reiterate Cézanne's geometric ideal. In *Woman with a Coffee Pot* Hortense's face is replaced by the heavy-set, wrinkled one of a Provençal housemaid, with her large, prehensile hands highlighted in the foreground. This figure is integrated in a finely orchestrated setting accentuated by the cylindrical coffee pot and the vertical line of the spoon in the tall cup. Cézanne's son Paul, who had become an important part of the artist's life, was the model together with Louis Guillaume for *Mardi Gras*, a canvas with the stock *Commedia dell'Arte* characters Harlequin and Pierrot in exaggerated, solemn poses, while the dominating elements are the tonal relationships between the setting and the figures. Even when *Harlequin* is painted by himself, the boy's features are translated into psychological fixity, and the definition of pictorial space reigns supreme.

The most important series of paintings that raised pictorial elements to a symbolic level was *The Card Players*, five canvases for which Cézanne executed numerous studies of individual figures. According to Paul Alexis, Cézanne had farmers in the Jas de Bouffan estate pose for these works, and the settings were the nearby farmhouses. The Barnes Foundation version, with five figures, is the largest, and is second in size only to *The Large Bathers*, with which it shares the bluish hues that lend symbolic value to space and figures alike. This version is considered the closest to a genre-type canvas because of the greater wealth of narrative details; but this opinion is belied by the monumentality and the colour, which have nothing naturalistic about them. The second version with four figures, kept at the Metropolitan Museum of Art, was followed by three others with only two figures. The farmers in the Barnes version posed separately for the painting and were later incorporated into the large canvas. But Cézanne was not at all interested in portraiture here, and although the figures certainly have character and one is tempted to attribute personalities to them, it is clear that they were chosen to convey more universal formal and expressive aims. The lack of depth, the few elements in the background and the irregular perspective of the table highlight the players – wrapped in clothes with rigid, voluminous folds accentuated by the players' large rounded shoulders and ungainly hands – in an unusually magniloquent manner. If the standing figure has less spatiality and seems to be absorbed by the wall, the others, including the child with her lovely oval face, are weighty and solid. Despite the gravity of the figures, the colour, applied with regular, masterful brushstrokes, imparts great unity to the canvas.

In *The Card Players* with four figures, Cézanne has dispensed with the game board, which was a colourful and decorative element in the preceding version, and focuses more on the game itself. But on the whole this work is not on the same level as the other, in which the presence of the child serves to enhance the gravity of the silent world of adults who are so intensely concentrated on their game in an enclosed space.

This motif had famous precedents and was even adopted by Impressionist artists such as Caillebotte. In Cézanne's case the most obvious source was the Le Nain brothers' canvas kept in the Granet Museum in Aix. He took the prototypes from the painting of the past, eliminating all immediate interpretative connotations (as Chardin had done before him) and any categorical naturalistic aims, thus elaborating a new painting genre.

In the three versions with two figures, the men seen in profile are placed at opposite sides of the table; the setting is starker, as Cézanne does away with the accessories in favour of essentiality, which Roger Fry described as "the gravity, the reserve and the weighty solemnity of some monument of antiquity." The frontal arrangement, dominated by the figures, is articulated in a harmonious rapport with the low-key colours in the background, while the structure of the tablecloth prevails with its imperiously chiselled folds. This enigmatic image, which has been analyzed in detail many times, retains its impenetrable quality.

Contemplation, concentration and essentiality converge to create an indestructible equilibrium. Much has been said about the contrast between the men's expressions, the one guarded and the other more open – a contrast that is reflected in their posture, features and even the shape of their hats. But the solemnity of these canvases is such as to permit the artist to place human beings in a higher order of harmonious relations.

In the series of four oil paintings and two watercolours of a *Boy with a Red Waistcoat*, Cézanne achieves a remarkable level of formal and psychological penetration. Painted in various poses, with his introspective air of melancholy reverie, the adolescent (who was a professional model from Italy, Michelangelo di Rosa) always has the same clothes: a white shirt, blue tie, brown trousers and a gaudy red waistcoat with a high lapel. He was painted standing facing the spectator, one hand on his hip and the other hanging beside his body in a pose of abandon halfway between movement and immobility; or in profile, with a meditative look, his face heightened by the line of a curtain which acts as a sort of counterpoint to his features; or again, he was portrayed with even more intense melancholy with his bent head resting on his hand. Some critics think that the poses were influenced by old masters: the studied elegance of Bronzino and Tuscan Mannerism in the case of the standing position, and the severe beauty of a Renaissance profile and thoughtful detachment of a Sibyl by Michelangelo for the other poses. In the different versions of the waistcoat, Cézanne takes obvious pleasure in modulating it in relation to the green shadows of the white shirt and the dark colours of the wall and curtain; by thus harmonizing the entire canvas around a single chromatic element and manipulating the motif in varied poses and settings, he establishes a new pictorial register and dimension.

Nudes are the other important motif in this period. After executing *Five Female Bathers* (1885-87), Cézanne concentrated on groups of males in natural settings until 1895. The *Bathers* at the Musée d'Orsay (1892-94) is Cézanne's highest achievement up to this time both in terms of artistic conception and because of the quality of the figures and the elimination of all narrative elements. Freed from the pyramidal construction of the earlier versions of bathers, the nudes are now set in a more open setting, a sort of elongated semicircle. In *Five Female Bathers* the deliberate ugliness of the grotesque and summarily rendered figures discourages psychological involvement on the part of the spectator, whereas here the physical barrier of the statuary nude males with their arms raised, counterbalanced by the geometric articulation of the white drapery, prevents us from penetrating the scene. Being well acquainted with the formal evolution of a work does not always help one to clarify its meaning. Some critics say that the point of departure for an interpretation of Cézanne's male nudes in a natural setting is the lyrical evocation of his adolescence, and in effect it is not difficult to find traces of nostalgia and the remoteness of time in them. Other theories have been expounded in this regard, from the artist's interest in the classical values of ancient relief to an unconscious manifestation of latent homosexuality.

In this period Cézanne resumed the bathers motif in a less aggressive manner than he had displayed ten years before, a sign of greater serenity both in his art and life. Previously, the male nudes were interpreted as a representation of his isolation, his frustrations, and his being misunderstood and rejected by his father, Zola, the Salon and the artistic milieus. This attitude gave way to resignation to his solitude, which is so admirably depicted in the central nude of the Musée d'Orsay canvas.

A continuity with *Five Female Bathers* can be noted in the evolution of certain female figures into male bathers. The standing nude at right, who seems to be waving to someone, stemmed from academic drawings, from Michelangelo to Delacroix; Lionello Venturi speaks of El Greco's influence; and one could say the same about the different baptism scenes by Signorelli or Andrea del Sarto. Furthermore, Cézanne owned a plaster cast of *The Flayed Man* by Houdon, and the central figure in the *Bathers* may very well have been inspired by Couture's *Romans of the Decadence*.

In the later versions of bathers some of the figures acquire a sort of sinuous counterpoint effect; rotating their hips to the left, the individual bodies appear more isolated and sometimes some of the aggressive features of the earliest bathing scenes come to the surface again. No sooner do the female bathers reappear, than sex once again becomes ambiguous and Cézanne moves towards the universality of the *Large Bathers*. The artist has placed these nudes, who are about to go into the water, in an Arcadian setting, a landscape marked by strong colour contrasts in an overall movement that is counterbalanced by the mass of white clouds. Cézanne is probably alluding to the two-fold nature of water, sacred and profane: purification through the holy water of baptism, and the festive immersion in a natural element that is a source of life.

172

♦ *Above left:*
Harlequin,
c. 1888-90.
Oil on canvas,
92 × 65 cm
(36 1/4 × 25 5/8 in).
Mr and Mrs Paul
Mellon Collection,
Upperville, Virginia.

♦ *Above right:*
Harlequin, *c. 1888.*
Pencil,
47.3 × 30.9 cm
(18 5/8 × 12 1/8 in).
Art Institute,
Chicago.

♦ *Opposite:* Mardi
Gras, *1888.*
Oil on canvas,
102 × 81 cm
(40 1/8 × 31 7/8 in).
Pushkin Museum,
Moscow. A subject
that lends itself to a
narrative treatment
becomes a pretext
for purely pictorial
experimentation.
Cézanne uses
Harlequin's cane
to emphasize the
spatial depth and the
lozenge pattern in
the costume becomes
its very structural
framework and sets
the figure in a
statuary immobility.
The impassive faces
are like masks.

174

♦ Bridge on the Marne River at Créteil, 1888. *Oil on canvas, 71 × 90 cm (28 × 35 7/16 in). Pushkin Museum, Moscow. In this work Cézanne concentrates on rendering the transparent reflections, but in his hands they acquire a volumetric value. The colours reflected in the water are conceived as pure pictorial masses. The parallel brushstrokes merge the different parts of the canvas into a homogenous whole that suggests harmony and infinity.*

♦ The Banks of the
Marne River, c. 1888.
Oil on canvas,
65 × 81 cm
(25 5/8 × 31 7/8 in).
Hermitage Museum,
St Petersburg.

*In his lake and
watercourse motifs,
Cézanne always
painted the
reflections on
immobile,
translucent surfaces.*

♦ Bridge over a Pool,
c. 1888-90.
Oil on canvas,
64 × 79 cm
(25 1/8 × 31 1/8 in).
Pushkin Museum,
Moscow. The mystery
of nature becomes   *deeper in this maze*
of forms and
reflections that create
a penetrating
unitary vision
as the artist plumbs
the depths of the
universe.

♦ Kitcher Still Life,
1888-90.
Oil on canvas,
65 × 81 cm
(25 5/8 × 31 7/8 in).
Musée d'Orsay,
Paris.
Because of the
complexi.y of the
superimposed,
receding planes, this
work has a synthetic,
monumental
character. The
careful arrangement
of the pictorial
elements triggers
a dynamic impetus.

178

♦ *Left:* Still Life with
Sugar Bowl, Jug
and Fruit, *c. 1888-90.*
Oil on canvas,
61 × 90 cm
(24 × 35 7/16 in).
Hermitage Museum,
Moscow.
This work is
dominated by an
"artificiality" quite
removed from
Cézanne's early,
'natural' still lifes.
The tangible
sensuousness of the
fruit and objects
is no less real and
sincere, but they now
play a much more
important role in the
artist's more
ambitious pictorial
research.

♦ *Above:* Still Life
with Fruit and Vase,
c. 1888-90.
Oil on canvas,
46 × 55 cm
(18 1/8 × 21 5/8 in).
Courtauld Institute
Galleries, London.

♦ *Above:* Vases of Geraniums, *c. 1888-90. Watercolour, 31 × 29 cm (11 1/2 × 11 3/8 in). National Gallery of Art, Washington, DC.*

♦ *Opposite:* Vases of Flowers, *1888-90. Oil on canvas, 89 × 71 cm (35 × 28 in). Barnes Foundation, Merion, Pennsylvania.*

Lyricism is counterbalanced by monumental stability. The charm of the objects is in perfect harmony with their absolute nature. The most eloquent element in the disposition of the motif is the red cloth.

182

♦ The Bellevue Pigeon Tower, 1888-92. Oil on canvas, 64.1 × 80 cm (25 1/4 × 31 1/2 in). Museum of Art, Cleveland. In 1889 Renoir rented the Bellevue estate from Cézanne's brother-in-law Maxim Conil and the two artists painted the Arc river valley and the pigeon tower together. Cézanne's view acquires masterful compositional unity through a fluid and transparent fusion of the colours. The luminous vibrations, rather than attenuate the compactness of the overall structure, accentuate the unifying power of the composition.

♦ La Colline des Pauvres near Château Noir, *1888-95. Oil on canvas, 63 × 81 cm (24 7/8 × 31 7/8 in). Metropolitan Museum of Art, New York. In his maturity, Cézanne painted his* *favourite childhood haunts. It almost seems as if he evokes the emotions of his adolescence with the thick and masterful brushstrokes that take in every particle of nature, penetrating it by means of colour.*

184

♦ *Above:* Rocky Slope with Trees, *c. 1890.* *Watercolour,* *31 × 48 cm* *(11 1/2 × 18 7/8 in).* *Von der Heydt* *Museum, Wuppertal.*

♦ *Below:* Still Life, *c. 1890. Watercolour,* *12 × 21 cm* *(4 3/4 × 8 1/4 in).* *National Museum* *of Western Art,* *Tokyo.*

♦ *Above:* Boy with a Red Waistcoat, *1888-90. Watercolour, 45 × 31 cm (17 5/8 × 11 1/2 in).* Feilchenfeldt Collection, Zurich. After the death of his father Cézanne inherited a fair amount of money and could finally afford professional models. The artist portrayed the Italian model Michelangelo di Rosa six times from 1888 to 1890, which allowed him to concentrate on a figure in different positions and settings.

186

♦ *Above:* Still Life with Bottle and Fruit *c. 1890.*
Oil on canvas,
60 × 71 cm
(23 5/8 × 28 in).
Private Collection,
New York.

♦ *Opposite:* Madame Cézanne in the Conservatory, *1891-92.*
Oil on canvas,
92 × 73 cm
(36 1/4 × 28 3/4 in).
Metropolitan

Museum of Art,
New York.
Here the brushwork
is light: the head is
structured by means
of delicate colour
modulations and its
tilt harmonizes with

the slanting lines
of the wall, trees
and the body.
The foreground
and background are
united in the curve
of the trunk
and arms.

♦ *Left:* The Card
Players, *1890-92.*
Oil on canvas,
134 × 181 cm
(52 3/4 × 71 1/4 in).
Barnes Foundation,
Merion,
Pennsylvania.
Cézanne used the
same figures for this
work and the other
four canvases in the
series executed in
the first half of the
1890s. The Barnes
version is mirrored
almost identically
in the work at the
Metropolitan
Museum of Art,
except for the
presence of the child
in the former and
slight differences
in the men's poses.
These two versions
were executed before
the other three, which
have only two
players. The five
paintings underwent
a gradual process
of simplification
and distillation.

♦ *Above:* The Card
Players, *c. 1890-92.*
Oil on canvas,
65 × 81 cm
(25 5/8 × 31 7/8 in).
Metropolitan
Museum of Art,
New York.

190

♦ Man with a Pipe,
1890-92.
Oil on canvas,
92.5 × 73.5 cm
(36 7/16 × 29 in).
Pushkin Museum,
Moscow. Cézanne
carefully renders the
features of his model
without letting the
portrait become
naturalistic.

♦ Man with a Pipe,
1890-92. Oil on
canvas, 73 × 60 cm
(28 3/4 × 23 5/8 in).
Courtauld Institute
Galleries, London.

*These portraits
of a man with a pipe
were actually studies
for the more
elaborate series
of* The Card Players.

192

♦ Madame Cézanne,
1890-92. Oil on
canvas, 62 × 51 cm
(24 7/16 × 20 1/8 in).
Museum of Art,
Philadelphia.
This delicate, fragile
portrait was painted
with the
Impressionist spirit
– the face without
shadows against
a light background,
and the subtle
relationship of the
warm and cold hues
of the face with those
on the wall.

♦ Madame Cézanne,
c. 1890-92. Oil on
canvas, 46 × 38 cm
(18 1/8 × 15 in).
Museum of Art,
Philadelphia.

*A compact portrait
that is concentrated
in the oval face and
the regular features
which effect an ideal
symmetry.*

194

♦ Madame Cézanne
in a Yellow Chair,
1890-94. Oil on
canvas, 116 × 89 cm
(45 5/8 × 35 in).
Metropolitan
Museum of Art,
New York. Cézanne
achieves a new
synthesis between
figure and setting by
means of heightened
monumentality and
plastic values. The
colours – red, yellow
and various shades
of blue in the
background – are
suffused with a
crystal-clear light.

◆ Woman with a Coffee Pot, 1890-94. Oil on canvas, 130 × 97 cm (51 1/8 × 38 1/4 in). Musée d'Orsay, Paris. Cézanne pays more attention to the simplified plastic rendering of the forms than to any character study of the woman. With its vigorous structure, the portrait exemplifies Cézanne's famous statement: "Drawing and colour are not separate and distinct, since everything in nature has colour. While one paints, one draws; the more the colour harmonizes, the more precise becomes the drawing. When the colour is rich, the form is at its height."

196

♦ Portrait of a Farmer, *1890-92. Oil on canvas, 55 × 46 cm (21 5/8 × 18 1/8 in). Hahnloser Collection, Bern. In his paintings of farmers at the Jas de Bouffan estate, Cézanne achieved a sort of characterization of human types, handling the poses and attitudes with naturalness. The plastic rhythm of the face, neck and clothes is particularly striking.*

◆ Male Bathers.
1892-94.
Oil on canvas,
60 × 82 cm
(23 5/8 × 32 1/4 in).
Musée d'Orsay,
Paris.
The figures are in an
open space, arranged
in the form of a
frieze, the tree in
the middle being the
axis. The man with
the cloth seems
to have been inspired
by a drawing
by Signorelli, and
Charles Sterling has
compared it to a
figure in El Greco's
Laocoon. This work
was exhibited at
the 1904 Salon
d'Automne and had
a great influence on
young artists such
as Denis, Matisse
and Picasso.

198

♦ *Above:* Boat and
Bathers, *1890-94.*
Oil on canvas,
30 × 124 cm
(11 3/4 × 48 3/4 in).
Musée de l'Orangerie,
Paris.

♦ *Right:* Madame
Cézanne in Red,
1890-94.
Oil on canvas,
89 × 70 cm
(35 × 27 1/2 in).
Museu de Arte,
São Paulo.

♦ Boy with a Red
Waistcoat, 1890-95.
Oil on canvas,
81 × 65 cm
(31 7/8 × 25 5/8 in).
Museum of Modern
Art, New York.
Cézanne portrayed
this model in four oil
paintings and two
watercolours, and
all the versions are
highly concentrated
works with deep
psychological
penetration.

200

♦ Houses at Bellevue,   *is important because*
c. 1890-94.   *of the clear-cut*
Oil on canvas,   *definition of the*
60 × 73 cm   *planes and the*
(23 5/8 × 28 3/4 in).   *free-moving touch*
Private Collection,   *the artist adopted*
Geneva. This work   *to render the foliage.*

◗ House and Trees,
1890-94.
Oil on canvas,
65.2 × 81 cm
(24 5/8 × 31 7/8 in).
Barnes Foundation,
Merion,
Pennsylvania
Cézanne loved
to paint the isolated
*farmhouses near
Aix surrounded
by trees that were
protected from the
mistral. This motif
was a sign of man's
harmony with
nature and the
artist's love for
simple things.*

♦ Still Life with
a Basket of Apples,
1890-94.
Oil on canvas,
60 × 80 cm
(23 5/8 × 31 1/2 in).
Art Institute,
Chicago.
This is a carefully
structured still life,
yet it seems casual,
natural, with
striking imbalance
in the details. The
overall equilibrium
seems to be more the
work of the artist
than an imitation of
an already existing,
natural stability.

206

♦ Four Male Bathers, 1890-1900. Oil on canvas, 22 × 35.5 cm (8 5/8 × 14 in): Musée d'Orsay, Paris. The typical group of bathers is handled here in a concise manner, with rapid, impetuous brushstrokes that lend a great deal of vibrancy to the work.

207

♦ Bathers, *c. 1890-92.*
Oil on canvas,
52 × 63 cm
(20 7/16 × 24 7/8 in).
St. Louis Art
Museum, St. Louis.
Although the poses
of the well-defined,
solidly built figures
resemble statues,
their dynamic vigour
integrates them
into the natural
setting.

♦ Boy with a Red
Waistcoat, *1890-95.*
Oil on canvas,
79 × 64 cm
(31 1/8 × 25 1/8 in).
Private Collection,
Switzerland.
An Italian model
gave Cézanne the
opportunity to create
a series of paintings
and drawings in
which he represents
the melancholy
and charm of this
adolescent in
formally balanced
compositions.

209

♦ The Card Players, 1892-96. Oil on canvas, 47 × 57 cm (18 1/2 × 22 3/4 in). Musée d'Orsay, Paris. Everything in this canvas is a pretext for a careful study of lines and volumes. The division of the space into two symmetrical areas emphasizes the contraposition of the players. The great simplification eliminates those narrative aspects typical of genre painting and leads to the abandonment of traditional perspective.

♦ *Above:* Still Life
with Ginger Jar and
Eggplants, *1890-94.*
Oil on canvas,
73 × 92 cm
(28 3/4 × 36 1/4 in).
Metropolitan
Museum of Art,
New York.

♦ *Opposite above:*
Houses and Field at
Bellevue, *c. 1892-95.*
Oil on canvas,
36 × 50 cm
(14 1/8 × 19 5/8 in).
Phillips Collection,
Washington, DC.

♦ *Opposite below:*
Bibémus, *1894-95.*
Oil on canvas,
71.5 × 89.8 cm
(28 1/8 × 35 3/8 in).
Solomon R.
Guggenheim
Museum, New York.

212

♦ Rocks, 1894-98.
Oil on canvas,
73 × 93 cm
(28 3/4 × 36 5/8 in).
Metropolitan
Museum of Art,
New York.
An impenetrable
terrain filled with
obstacles conveys a
sensation of violence
and desolation.

From the rocks
there emerge trunks
with light foliage, the
pale and distant sky
is empty,
immaterial.
The horizon line
that establishes
the spectator's
viewpoint, fades
away amidst the
trees and rocks.

213

♦ Rocks in the Forest,
c. 1890-98.
Oil on canvas,
48.5 × 59.5 cm
(19 1/16 × 23 7/16
in). Kunsthaus,
Zurich.
According to
Joaquim Gasquet,
Cézanne said:
"Nature is always the
same, and yet
its appearance
is always changing.
It is our business
as artists to convey
the thrill of nature's
permanence along
with the elements
and the appearance
of all its changes.
Painting must give
us the flavour of
nature's eternity."

A Harmony Parallel to Nature

The many noteworthy, innovative achievements in the last decade of Cézanne's production are marked by a fragmented, disconnected brushstroke and increasing detachment from sense perception, as well as by the autonomous nature of the pictorial surface dominated by extremely articulated colour modulation. The result was not so much an image of nature, as "a harmony parallel to nature", as Cézanne himself stated. Joachim Gasquet said he had heard the artist speak of the need to grasp and harmonize "nature seen out there [showing Gasquet the green and blue plain] and nature felt in here [touching his forehead], since they must merge in order to last and to live a life that is half human and half divine [...] the life of art."

Watercolours proved to be a useful aid in finding certain means for his new pictorial procedure. The fact that his canvases are often unfinished, that some surface areas are not painted in, and that natural elements become attenuated, almost insubstantial, in space, is partly the result of his working in watercolour: this is a medium that requires transparent colour and no hesitation or pentimenti, a means whereby the artist makes void sublime by transforming blank areas into structural elements, into space. Cézanne anticipates that taste for lightness and the essential gesture so typical of contemporary art (James Joyce would have called it a "work in progress") which can also be seen clearly in his many versions of a single theme, which is a sign of creative torment and ideal tension on the part of an artist who was determined to vie with Poussin, Veronese, Delacroix and Courbet.

Naturally, given Cézanne's complex and contradictory nature, this new feeling of lightness was counterbalanced, in his final years, by thicker colour (e.g. some portraits of Vallier and the *Mont Sainte-Victoire Seen from Les Lauves* in the Pushkin Museum in Moscow). Colour becomes the absolutely dominant element through which the artist, by means of a series of carefully controlled modulations, seeks to interpret nature through his 'eye and mind.' The path

towards the disintegration of the object in some of the most memorable works of an artist who was so passionately attached to material consistency and volume, is the hallmark of the attraction and unfathomable nature of Cézanne's final works, as Lawrence Gowing says. As we have seen, while his Impressionist friends were rendering the effect of light and atmosphere, he was painting objects, but in his final period the physical aspects of the world blended more and more in the flow of colour.

As Lilian Brion Guerry has demonstrated, Cézanne was the author of the break with traditional spatial composition which gave rise to all modern painting, from Cubism to Expressionism and non-figurative art. His space was no longer the cube of air in which the volumes were arranged according to a pre-established order. Unlike the composition bound to the Renaissance rules of perspective and the techniques adopted to achieve it – which, despite the Baroque 'transfigurations,' prevailed until Impressionism – in Cézanne the spatial 'container' does not precede its 'contents,' nor are the two distinct. By spreading and taking on form in the third dimension, the object – be it a part of a landscape, a still life or a human figure – calls forth from itself the structure that gives it an identity. It is therefore indissolubly linked to the spatial configuration it creates: together they form a new, transcending unity. Cézanne sought to find a balance between the violence of sensation and the creation of a new harmony – though until the end he was never sure he had reached his goal. Sensations lie at the heart of his art, they were always his pride and joy and the justification for all his striving; but in his final years he tended to record them like something organized in a rational logic. He despised every movement in which 'the eye directs the hand without the aid of reason.' His fits of anguish worsened, as did his fear that old age would not permit him to accomplish what he had constantly pursued. He began to compare himself to Moses: "Shall I ever reach the Promised Land?"

he wrote to his son a week before his death. "I cannot attain the intensity that is unfolded before my senses. I do not have the magnificent richness of colouring that animates nature." In the works of his first decade of production, the composition was governed by prevalently literary inspiration and motifs, and the canvases were more informed by psychological content than plastic values; the contrast of light and shadow, the surface animated and agitated by feverish brushstrokes and applications with the palette knife, were more important at that time than finding an inner rhythm that could unify space and objects. This conflict seems to be dominated in his so-called Impressionist period, when the faithful recording of sense perception also implied the mobility and transience of his colour and light combinations, while the atmosphere was the stabilizing element, since Cézanne was interested in capturing the ineffable and making it durable, in "making Impressionism into something as solid and permanent as the art in museums."

Cézanne felt the inadequacy of the approach that set out to isolate one instant of sense perception from the constant spatial-temporal flow of nature. He therefore tried to synthesize the sequence of sensations by creating a superior order and harmony through rational analysis. Frustration and problems were inevitable: caused on the one hand by the fragmentation of form due to light, and on the other because the preponderance of volume brought about a lack of spatial unity – to the detriment of the overall organic unity. Nevertheless, during his Impressionist period he executed some fine works. With the human figure Cézanne sometimes succeeds in conveying, in highly complex ways, the variety of expressions that animate a face in harmony with the light vibrations and that impart vitality to the surrounding space. Or the different elements in a still life are connected in such a way as to harmonize the tonal variations. A subtle equilibrium is established between the container and the contents, an arduous harmony among diverse elements.

At a certain stage Cézanne again addresses the problem of spatial unity from a different angle, as it were, by seeking a common essence and fusing solid elements, not in a single construction but on abstract planes. This gives rise, from the late 1870s to the mid-1890s, to series such as *L'Estaque*, the first *Mont Sainte-Victoire* and *Gardanne* canvases, the *Card Players* and some *Bathers*. The plastic value of the object determines its position in space and becomes the very *raison d'être* of its equilibrium. Since it was impossible to reproduce the complexity of details, Cézanne became selective, choosing from among the various natural data, simplifying, creating those harmonies parallel to nature he so doggedly pursued. He therefore effected an equilibrium, which was perhaps even more stable than the natural harmony that had inspired him. There are no longer atmospheric effects that can alter facial features and the plastic stability of a landscape or undermine the integrity of the fruit and objects in the large-size still lifes.

The structural unity of the composition is thus achieved. There are no longer elements in heterogeneous nature striving to be merged in a dynamic impetus as in his early works, nor do these elements struggle against potential fragmentation as in the Auvers landscape; now both the solid and unstable components have become a plastic or homogeneous, inseparable mass. In these new compositions, if in only one point on the canvas the formal structure is not clearly indicated, or the tonal value is too weak or too saturated – the entire work becomes dissonant, imbalanced. To be sure, this is a difficult equilibrium to attain, a fine line of reconciliation between the sensations aroused by reality and the stimuli of the imagination. The formal simplification of the object is the prelude to independent reconstruction, which obliges the artist to work around a play of abstract combinations that are established as a self-sustaining structural system. The world of representation is transformed into a complex whole consisting of combinations of volumes, the disposition of which is subordinate to the artist's will. A will that is arbitrary for those who have always said that nature is their primary model, since the world of images must forge the conditions of its own equilibrium, which vary according to the data and elements of each spatial combination. Hence the anomalies in construction, the masterful play of compensated imbalance that the artist must utilize in order to ensure the stability of his creation.

In order to solve this problem, a new technical procedure was necessary, a tangible sign of an aesthetic 'revolution.' The solution adopted by the Cubists was to obtain more rigorous spatial unity by compressing the components, and the space itself, into a pictorial armature that was deliberately made autonomous and was, however, still patterned after the visible, concrete world. The Cubists enlivened the canvas by representing objects on a flat surface in three dimensions through the simultaneous rendering of their different facets. But for Cézanne the results achieved in *Woman with a Coffee Pot*, who is frozen in an abstract space, or in the houses in *Gardanne*, which have become inalterable cubes and prisms, were unsurpassable limits.

He remained a 19th-century artist, far removed from the paths art took a short time before, and immediately after, his death – though he did serve as a catalyst for these and other artistic movements by opening many routes in pictorial procedure.

Another possible solution was to forgo three-dimensionality, the 'playing card' type of landscape that Cézanne had seen for the first time at L'Estaque in 1877. But this path was also unfeasible for an artist who observed nature more in depth than on the surface. He therefore had to tackle compositional problems in a different manner: no longer through the reduction of forms into volumes, but by creating them afresh in their essential freedom, which included movement, uncertainty, modulation – in other words, life. Thus, the object that until then had been characterized by the clarity of its outline and by its

rigorously self-contained volume, once again became receptive to the vibrations of atmosphere. Naturally this was a dynamic process that was attained gradually and not without contradictions; the works executed before the end of the century are often similar, as regards form, to those of the preceding years. But the large still lifes became more impressive and powerful, more deliberately systematic; the drapery falls grandiosely over the pictorial plane; the colour is intense and deep, occasionally extreme, rich in echoes and vibrations that permeate the entire canvas. At times the still lifes seem to be indoor landscapes, the rumpled folds of the tablecloth and carpet look like a mountain, evoking the shape of Mont Sainte-Victoire (*Still Life with Apples and Oranges*, 1895-1900; *Still Life with Water Jug*, 1899).

Still Life with Apples at the Museum of Modern Art in New York (1895-98) has an unfinished quality: the surface with little paint contrasts with Cézanne's habit of creating surfaces that appear to be almost in relief because of their impasto. Important areas are covered with a thin layer of pigment and this lack of density clashes with, and is counterbalanced by, the prominent objects on the table. The colours are the linchpin of the structure of the canvas. The complexity of the subject and compositional solidity of *Still Life with Plaster Cupid* (1895) are striking, as it has none of the incongruities typical of the picture within a picture, and the Baroque sculpture, everyday objects and painterly qualities are perfectly blended. *Still Life with Bottle and Onions* (1896-98) is a captivating work in which the brushstrokes are thicker and more vibrant, the surface less smooth and the colours darker – which show how Cézanne was seeking to realize that unique approach to nature that was to mark his last period.

Already in *Portrait of Gustave Geffroy* (1895) we note a sort of liberation from traditional patterns that he achieves through rich and modulated colours. When Geffroy watched Cézanne painting he saw how he built

up tiny layers of colour, modulating them with infinite patience so that the canvas always had a fresh, luminous quality. He superimposed a variable and variegated colour over an armature that was still somewhat geometrical; the pigment is quite thin, especially on the face.

As Roger Fry said, we cannot but admire Cézanne's capacity to organize such disparate objects with utter assurance and solidity and to dominate such a complicated network of movement and plastic tension by means of colour. According to the English critic, Cézanne was the first modern artist to conceive a means of organizing the complexity of appearance without imposing a priori patterns, thus giving it an interpretation that was the fruit of long contemplation. There is nothing that suggests a mechanical process, every trace of harshness is eliminated in the harmony established between rigorous intelligence and keen sensitivity that concur to give the impression of a living reality.

In the *Portrait of Joaquim Gasquet* as well, the hair is barely sketched and the face is rendered with a thin layer of pink, yellows, and pale blues. The 'watercolour' technique mentioned by many of the artist's models – from Geffroy to Vollard – is quite evident here. The diluted dabs of colour are transparent; the image is created by means of successive brushstrokes, and when the artist wants to model by 'modulating' he applies the colour in diaphanous layers. In *Portrait of Ambroise Vollard* (1899) the composition, aligned on inflexible axes, is solidified by means of the colour, which makes the form emerge in vertical areas. The colour correspondences are actually conceived as a merging of forms; areas where the paint is applied more thickly, in which Cézanne wants to separate the volumes from the flat background, alternate with other areas rendered with the 'watercolour' technique.

Self-portrait with Beret (1899-1900), Cézanne's last work in this genre, is also animated by light brushstrokes. His expression has none of the fiery energy that characterized his preceding self-portraits; his calm,

distant gaze lends a virtually abstract air to his face, in which flat, almost immaterial surfaces are placed over one another in perfect equilibrium. In this severe, detached image, the features created with painstaking and masterful brushstrokes belong to an artist who after years of hardship and frustration has learned that withdrawal, isolation and dignity are the keys to his artistic vigour. The second half of the 1890s are dominated by the landscapes of the Bibémus quarry – chaotic, primordial elements that Cézanne transforms into logical pictorial planes. In the suffocating heat and intense light he found a nature that shared his human suffering. Lionello Venturi has rightly said that the views of Bibémus invite comparison to Dante's Inferno. *The Red Rock* is characterized by the dramatic relationship between the masses of trees rendered with short brushstrokes and the interruption of the overhanging rock face. *Mont Sainte-Victoire Seen from the Bibémus Quarry* has a series of massive, tortuous rock formations with intense orange hues that stand out imposingly in the landscape, relating to the green vegetation and blue sky, which occupies very little space in uppermost part of the canvas. In this powerful work the artist has placed a gully between the spectator and the principal motif, an abyss beyond which rise the rocks and the majestic peak of the mountain, looming in the background like an epic sculpture. The profile of Sainte-Victoire is created through a series of tonal contrasts that transfigure the motif into a variegated texture of correspondences in a free play of forms and colours. The modulated structure integrates the artist's sensations into a unified assemblage of pictorial elements: the real innovation in Cézanne's technique lies in his modulation of colour. The values of representation and the spatial, surface and light values merge and interact in solidly structured units. The colours – used as a vehicle for pulsating tension and passion – rise from the center of the earth, they are the very life of ideas; applied in short, parallel strokes, they saturate the canvas, lending it depth and intensity.

216

♦ Portrait of Gustave
Geffroy, c. 1895.
Oil on canvas,
116 × 89 cm
(45 5/8 × 35 in).
Private Collection.
"Cézanne was the
first modern painter
to conceive a means
of organizing the
infinite complexity
of appearance in a
geometric structure,"
said Roger Fry. The
writer Geffroy had
liberal ideas, and
wrote a biography
of the socialist Louis-
Auguste Blanqui,
whereas Cézanne
became more and
more conservative
as he grew older; yet
their friendship was
marked by mutual
esteem, as Geffroy's
penetrating art
criticism shows.

217

♦ Self-portrait,
c. 1895 Watercolour,
28 × 26 cm
(11 × 19 1/4 in).
Feilchenfeldt

Collection, Zurich.
The French Cubist
painter André Lhote
said: "Cézanne has
the talent to establish

the essence of a
person. This eye,
reddened because it
has peered into the
imponderable for too

long a time, was able
to discover – under
the variations of the
skin – the plastic
signs of inner life."

♦ *Left:* Large Pine and Red Earth, *c. 1895.*
Oil on canvas,
73 × 92 cm
(28 3/4 × 36 1/4 in).
Hermitage Museum,
St. Petersburg.
The gigantic pine
almost completely
obscures the
landscape.
The choice of the
golden section for
the vertical and
horizontal axes
underscores the
monumentality
of this canvas, once
again demonstrating
how Cézanne finds
an almost sacred
spirit in nature.

♦ *Above:* Still Life with Bottle and Onions, *c. 1895.*
Oil on canvas,
66 × 82 cm
(26 × 32 1/4 in).
Musée d'Orsay,
Paris.
"Yes, go ahead and
draw," Cézanne said
in 1905, "but it is
light that envelops
things, light with
its general reflection
is their container."
The objects in this
canvas, viewed from
different angles,
foreshadow the
Cubist approach
to spatial
configuration.

220

♦ *Above:* Still Life
with Plaster Cupid,
1895. Oil on canvas,
63 × 81 cm
(24 7/8 × 31 7/8 in).
Nationalmuseum,
Stockholm.

♦ *Opposite:* Still Life
with Plaster Cupid,
1895. Oil on canvas,
70 × 57 cm
(27 1/2 × 22 3/4 in).
Courtauld Institute
Galleries, London.

222

♦ *Opposite above:*
Still Life with Apples,
1895-98.
Oil on canvas,
68.6 × 92.7 cm
(27 × 36 1/2 in).
Museum of Modern
Art, New York.

♦ *Opposite below:*
Still Life with Apples
and Oranges,
1895-1900.
Oil on canvas,
74 × 93 cm
(29 1/8 × 36 5/8 in).
Musée d'Orsay,
Paris. The space is
dialectical, the
difference between
depth and surface,
horizontal and
vertical planes,
is decreased.
Everything moves

forwards, towards
the spectator, without
sacrificing any of the
depth. The continuity
of the elements is
more complex, and
the surface is filled
with unexpected
forms and colour
harmonies, almost
to the saturation
point. Yet this
fantastic cluster
of objects is carefully
and tastefully
organized.

♦ *Above:* Still Life
with Water Jug,
1895.1900.
Oil on canvas,
53 × 71 cm
(20 7/8 × 28 in).
Tate Gallery,
London.

224

♦ *Above:* Foliage,
*1895-1900. Pencil
and watercolour,
44 × 65 cm
(17 3/8 × 25 5/8 in).
Museum of Modern
Art, New York.*

♦ *Opposite above:*
Provençal Landscape,
*c. 1895-1900.
Watercolour,
31 × 48 cm
(11 1/2 × 18 7/8 in).
Szépmüvészeti
Múzeum, Budapest.*

♦ *Opposite below:*
Rock Wall over
the Château Noir,
*c. 1895-1900.
Watercolour and
pencil,
31.7 × 47.6 cm
(12 1/2 × 18 3/4 in).
Museum of Modern
Art, New York.*

*This extremely
simple work reveals
Cézanne's formidable
perception and
execution in
revealing a world
with a few barely
sketched, almost
surreptitious, signs
on the paper.*

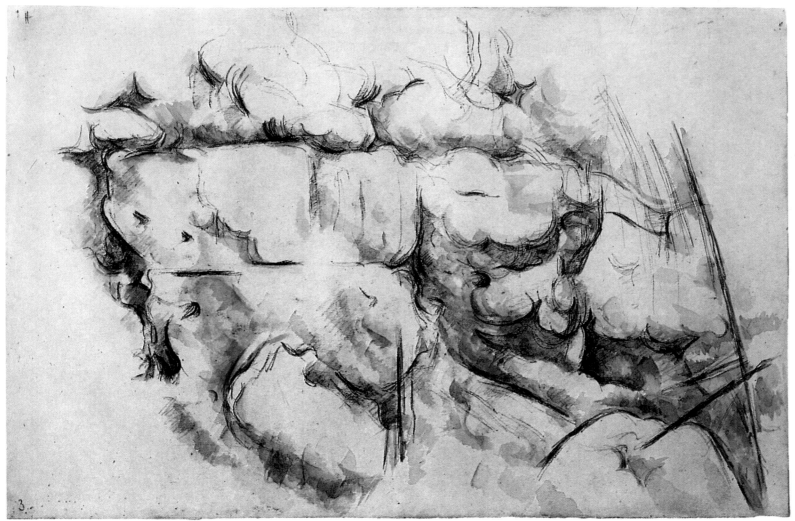

226

♦ Mont Sainte-Victoire Seen from the Road to Tholonet, 1896-98. Oil on canvas, 81 × 100 cm (31 7/8 × 39 3/8 in). Hermitage Museum, St. Petersburg. The majestic mountain is not situated in the landscape; it is the landscape. "I go right up to the motif and lose myself in it," Cézanne stated. Mont Sainte-Victoire dominates the scene in a clear light in which continuous, conflicting variations move up to the light area of the sky. Cézanne's space is an area permeated by tension, the rhythm of which imparts a formal dimension to the various pictorial elements in free-moving bursts of energy.

♦ Lake Annecy, *1896.*
Oil on canvas,
64.2 × 79.1 cm
(25 1/4 × 31 1/8 in).
Home House
Trustees, London.
This magnificent
work, painted by

Cézanne during
a sojourn in
Switzerland in
which he sorely
missed his Provençal
landscape, is
transformed into an
impenetrable prism.

228

♦ Mont Sainte-
Victoire Seen from
the Bibémus Quarry,
c. 1897. Oil on
canvas, 65 × 81 cm
(25 5/8 × 31 7/8 in).
Museum of Art,
Baltimore.
The gully formed
by the quarry in the
foreground separates
the mountain from
the spectator (though
it still looms over
the foreground),
creating a dramatic
scene filled with
conflicting forces.
The greens unify
the separate planes;
the orange rocks
and blue sky,
rendered with strong
contrasts, connect
the foreground and
background.

229

♦ Forest Interior, 1898-99. Oil on canvas, 61 × 81 cm (24 × 31 7/8 in) California Palace of the Legion of Honor, San Francisco. Cézanne's choice of a wild scene without a horizon from which man is excluded, testifies to his total identification with nature, an approach that can be likened to Monet's Water Lily series.

230

♦ *Above:* Portrait
of Joaquim Gasquet,
1896-97.
Oil on canvas,
65.6 × 73.5 cm
(25 7/8 × 29 in).
Národní Galerie,
Prague.

♦ *Opposite:* Boy with
Skull, *1896-98.*
Oil on canvas,
130.2 × 97.3 cm
(51 1/4 × 38 3/8 in).
Barnes Foundation,
Merion,
Pennsylvania.
The palette is

dominated by
a subtle range of
purple, cobalt blue
and green in which
the white of the pages
and the skull stand
out. The melancholy
boy is the picture
of youth as opposed

to death. The skull,
which serves to
reminds us of our
mortality, is a
common motif in
Western art, both
in still lifes and
compositions with
figures.

232

♦ Peasant with a Blue
Blouse, c. 1897.
Oil on canvas,
80 × 63.5 cm
(31 1/2 × 25 in).
Kimbell Art Museum,
Fort Worth.

♦ Seated Peasant,
c. 1900. Watercolour,
22 × 32 cm
(8 5/8 × 12 3/8 in).
Kunsthaus, Zurich.

♦ *Above:* Study for
"Large Bathers,"
*c. 1989-1905. Oil on
canvas, 73 × 92 cm
(28 3/4 × 36 1/4 in).
Feilchenfeldt
Collection, Zurich.*

♦ *Below:* Seven
Bathers, *c. 1900.
Oil on canvas,
37.5 × 45.5 cm
(14 3/4 × 18 in).
Beyeler Galerie,
Basle.*

234

♦ *Above:* Portrait of Ambroise Vollard, *1899. Oil on canvas, 100.3 × 81.2 cm (39 1/2 × 32 in). Musée du Petit Palais, Paris. Cézanne's art dealer* patiently submitted to 115 sittings for this portrait, but despite this the pigment is rather thinly applied, except for the face, shoulders, neck *and jacket collar, where the artist wanted to heighten the volumes.*

♦ *Opposite:* Self-portrait with Beret, *1898-1900. Oil on canvas, 63.5 × 50.8 cm (25 × 20 in). Museum of Fine Arts, Boston.*

236

♦ Still Life with
Curtain, Jug and
Fruit, c. 1899. Oil on
canvas, 54 × 73 cm
(21 1/4 × 28 3/4 in).
Hermitage Museum,
St. Petersburg.
Although some of
his admirers accuse
him of a lack
of imagination,
Cézanne
demonstrates
considerable
inventiveness when
he uses the same
objects to create
a series of still lifes
in which each object
plays a different
a role. Without ever
repeating the
arrangement,
he achieves new
equilibrium
and spatial
correspondences,
new colour
harmonies,
by grouping the
objects in a truly
extraordinary
variety of
compositions.

♦ Flowers, c. 1900.
Oil on canvas,
77 × 64 cm
(30 3/8 × 25 1/8 in).
Pushkin Museum,
Moscow.
This work is a copy
of a watercolour
by Delacroix, Roses
and Hydrangea,
which Cézanne
bought from Vollard
after the Chocquet
collection had been
auctioned off and
hung on the wall
of his house at Rue
Boulegon in Aix.

The Promised Land

In the works of his final period, Cézanne dispenses with the rigorous architecture of volumes and space, thus lending greater mobility to the images and offering more possibility for combinations of diverse elements. Now no longer placed in a restrictive context, the object contracts and expands according to the play of light, in a sort of vital pulsation. It is almost as if Cézanne were anxious to restore communication with the real world. In his still lifes he tends to abolish the rigidity of oversharp outlines and introduces the folds – which seem to be casual but are really quite carefully arranged – of dark, flowered cloth; he meditates on the fusion of planes, the mutual heightening of colours, and the harmonious correspondences among the different elements.

Still Life with Apples and Peaches (1905) has an absolutely autonomous spatial structure; each object serves to underscore a particular pictorial viewpoint. "The eye must absorb and concentrate, the mind must formulate." A series of formal relationships generates a play of tension between surface and depth. The most intense colour values are concentrated on the fruit, but an interaction of basic colours runs through the whole canvas. "Art is a religion. Its goal is the elevation of the spirit," Cézanne stated; his objects have become metaphors for a profound vision of the sensory world. Since in his portraits Cézanne sets out to place the image in time as well as in space, he tries to harmonize the mobility of the air with that of the person portrayed – a rather difficult task. A comparison between the portraits of his final period, especially those of his gardener Vallier, and *Card Players* and *Woman with a Coffee Pot*, shows the great difference between the figures isolated in timeless immobility and those harmonized with nature's rhythm, pulsation and nuances. By integrating figure and space, Cézanne works a miracle: he creates a representation that transcends the immediate sense datum and comes to life not by fragmentizing the figure absorbed by the reflections of an Impressionist type of light, but by penetrating it to the full. "Painting is not slavishly copying the object, it is seeking the harmony among different relationships."

The relationship between the volume and its collocation in the space that surrounds it is based on an undefined area – the mobility of which is its very *raison d'être* – situated between the ideal contours of the solid element and its representation. This imparts balance to the composition, a balance which, albeit momentary, is more important than any form of stability. By this means Cézanne achieves an ever more subtle and rare combination of his artistic will with the expression the work takes on through the spectator's imagination. The predominant note in these works is the artist's pursuit of a more dynamic and perfectible harmony by embracing and exploiting all the potential of an image. Spatial depth extends further and further in numerous directions by means of a series of elements that are suggested rather than explicitly rendered. This is a multiple space in which the object, instead of being presented as a self-contained volume, is re-created within the context of the new, deeper meanings it takes on.

Mont Sainte-Victoire is no longer isolated in its volumetric self-sufficiency, but is the mountain *par excellence*, set on a cosmic scale, transcending the visible aspect of the natural world, a projection of the inner space of the artist who created it. Cézanne senses the existence of a new consciousness of spatial structure in which objects open out to one other, interpenetrating without limits, a Promised Land which Cézanne, "like the great Hebrew leader," was afraid he would never enter. This stance is radically different from the heightening of form that inspired the Cubist aesthetic, which owed so much to Cézanne's redefinition of the picture plane and his emphasis on solidity and relief. The yearning for a cosmic, spiritual life so characteristic of Cézanne's new vision might even be considered a forerunner of historical non-figurative painting – from Klee to Kandinsky – that aims at representing a world without restrictions and seeks a free-ranging space in its attempt to extend the real beyond its figured appearances.

At the beginning of the 20th century Cézanne's works reveal more interest in texture and chromatic nuance. Through watercolours he discovered that by modulating colours and setting them in contrast he could suggest shifting planes and surfaces, and by ascending the chromatic scale at regular intervals he was able to define forms by reaching the culminating point and then descend in the opposite direction. "Contrasts and relations of tone, that is the secret of drawing and modelling," he said to Bernard. In the watercolour *Foliage* (1895-1900), for example, the colour contrast coincides with the inner life of the image.

The creation of form through colour modulation took a new, more physical and sensuous path in his paintings of the rocks at the Château Noir, which were the most important motifs in the first two or three years of this century. Flashes of sensuousness emanate from the masses of rock surrounding the château, thus demonstrating how the distinctive character of a place is able to create a disturbing physical presence, a mood, as it were. The inextricable web of boulders, bushes and trees offers a new series of motifs that lend themselves to the artist's meditation on the diversity and complexity of nature. This chaotic, irrational landscape generates a tangle of sensations. The deep tonalities of the underbrush at the Château Noir supplant the light, brilliant contrasts of orange, blue and emerald green at the Bibémus quarry, presenting a complex interpenetration of sienna and purple. The watercolours sometimes evoke the rhythmical sequences of Baroque sculpture: branches like large spirals of sculpted hair shoot outwards in a centrifugal burst of energy that is created totally through colour.

Cézanne tends more and more to interpret nature in terms of 'coloured spots' which, obeying a law of harmony, follow one another in structured sequences. In themselves these spots do not represent anything, but take on meaning through their relationships to one another – relationships of correspondence and contrast, progressions from tone to tone in a gamut of modulations that propose a representation parallel to the natural image. Their meaning lies in the juxtapositions and alignments, which not only create volumes but also principal axes that are perpendicular to the chromatic scales. When the relationships of tones are harmoniously juxtaposed, the canvas is modelled by itself. This is quite evident in the views of Mont Sainte-Victoire, the key motif of the artist's final production. Cézanne contemplated the mountain from several different viewpoints – the Bibémus quarry, the Château Noir, the Tholonet road, the hills of Les Lauves. Over the years the massive rock formation is seen at closer and closer range; through colour modulation and sequential mosaic-like brushstrokes he made the space a homogeneous unit, an interwoven fabric. From the beginning of the 1890s on he began using colour modulation to suggest depth. In the series painted at Les Lauves he revealed a new dimension of his art, utilizing the discovery of the pictorial homogeneity of space in landscape to render sensation, and not as a mere abstract theory of representation. The series probably begins with the version kept at the Nelson-Atkins Museum in Kansas City (1902-1906), in which the modelling in the foreground is tangible and the distant mountain is sculpted by means of angular brushstrokes, quite similar in style to those Cézanne adopted when he painted the other side of Mont Sainte-Victoire from the Tholonet road, from 1896 to 1898. In the Philadelphia Museum of Art version (*Mont Sainte-Victoire Seen from Les Lauves*, 1902-1904) we note he has separated the lower green and ochre area from the upper blue one dominated by the mountain; painting from a high viewpoint, Cézanne sets onto the vertical plane of the canvas a landscape that his glance embraces from the hill to the plain and then ascends once again along the sides of the mountain, so that the perceptive space seems to be concave. Having eliminated the sequence of receding planes, he now builds an austere rhythmic structure, a form that grows out of colour, dominated by a grandiose sense of pictorial harmony that is achieved by means of interacting forms. The subject extends over the entire surface, to the ends of the canvas; the wealth of colour gradations reveals Cézanne's temperament, his intelligence, tenacious will, and acute visual perception. He always worked on the overall effect of the different elements. He immersed himself totally in his painting precisely by painting. He watched the work grow slowly, dominated by the idea of its unfinished quality. Especially in the final years of his production, every canvas was a living entity that came into being step by step and that only death would be able to interrupt.

The version of *Mont Sainte-Victoire* at the Kunsthaus in Zurich (1902-04) is a mosaic of large spots of colour with attenuated tones that seem to have been applied at random – horizontally, vertically, diagonally. The thick blue of the sky is rent by harsh greens. It is amazing to see the multicoloured fragments interlock and become a unified whole when one moves away from the canvas, while the axes and planes break away in depth. Although this is not Seurat's method of applying tiny dots of colour, the effect is the same: it is impossible for the spectator to observe the canvas from close-up, as the eye needs distance to blend the colour and form the image. Here Cézanne is not interested in individual forms, since he is seeking an all-encompassing, 'abstract' vision, or at least an 'in-depth' vision. Behind the summary handling and the crust of pigment that is sometimes quite thick, there lies a deep understanding of, and identification with, nature – the fruit of a lifetime of dogged and humble striving and experience.

In the Basle Kunstmuseum version of *Mont Sainte-Victoire* (1904-06) Cézanne's creative torment takes on an almost tragic dimension which is attained through astonishing expressive power, intense colours and a higher scale of values. The network of coloured touches is thicker in this canvas; the landscape is suffused by a dark shadow that becomes quite thick in the middle of the plain and is somewhat attenuated in a finely wrought area of oranges, reds, ochres and browns and in the blue of the mountain. The dark green mass at left

seems impermeable to light and serves to highlight two distinct pictorial approaches – the quest for depth, and heightened surface values. In the Pushkin Museum version (1905-06), perhaps the last in the series, the paint is applied more thickly in closely related brushstrokes that carefully avoid any break in continuity, thus making the construction more solid and lending greater weight to the motif. The dense plain has lost its depth and has gained in verticality, in an area with innumerable glimmering facets that enhance the blacks, browns, greens and purples in a thick, complex harmony. The effect of depth is achieved by the majestic mountain that delimits the plain like a sort of horizon line. In the very heart of this powerful, passionately solemn canvas there is a patch of warm light, as if the sun had slipped away from the foot of the mountain. This is the last stage of his quest for pictorial mastery of the motif. The strata of overlaid colour lend a rich granular effect to the texture. The agitated, tense handling, abundance of material qualities and impassioned, vigorous brushstrokes justify the theory that this is the last view of Mont Sainte-Victoire seen from Les Lauves.

Cézanne's statement "I have sworn to myself to die painting" implies that he was ready to die for painting in order to make it live; there is a sense of his laying himself bare, as it were. He found himself at the final stage of a tradition and the beginning of a phase in which the very values of this tradition were being questioned. Sainte-Victoire rises up like a luminous object of desire, it is the image of a mirage, a sublime utopia immortalized in painting. In its plastic existence and harmonious perfection, the mountain is not so much the representation of nature as it is the visionary quest for, and dream of, nature: a harmony parallel to nature.

In his final years Cézanne again turned to the bathers motif, in particular the three large canvases kept at the Barnes Foundation, the National Gallery in London and the Philadelphia Museum of Art, which were probably executed at the same time, since Cézanne worked on them alternately on his huge easel at the Les

Lauves studio. These are monumental paintings that take up the theme of the nude in a natural setting and the harmony between man and nature, to which he had dedicated about two hundred works whose real meaning is often unclear.

Animated groups of figures that are a distant echo of *Le déjeuner sur l'herbe* are depicted in a moment of relaxation in varied poses. Cézanne drew inspiration from the centuries-old tradition of pastoral scenes which ranges from Raphael and Giorgione to Manet and Renoir; but his pictorial procedure is totally different. The Barnes Foundation version of *Large Bathers* has the most physical vitality and theatrical aura because of the great energy and intensity in the handling, the density of the colours and the emotionally charged, dramatic expression "with the branches of the trees that protrude like broken arrows and the conflicting light and shadows," as Lionello Venturi said.

The London version is noteworthy for its intense colours, the roughness of its surface, in which the figures are clearly delineated in black, and for the compressed, almost sculpturesque, energy of the figures with mask-like faces which are aligned vertically, as in a sarcophagus frieze.

The Philadelphia canvas, which is often considered the last in chronological order, has greater architectural solemnity, more subtle chromatic effects similar to those in watercolours, and an expressive monumentality of transcendental calm and grandeur. The figures are rendered with short brushstrokes, and the tonal contrasts create blocks of colours much like the ones in the landscapes Cézanne executed in the same period, in which houses, trees, and mountains are constructed by means of patches of colour. The form of the trees, like a pointed arch, is mirrored in the arms of the women in the middle foreground and heightened in the low horizon line and vast sky. A dreamy atmosphere is created by the predominating bluish hues; the rigidly structured composition is infused with a somewhat disturbing mood. The pronounced symmetry of this canvas, the nudes which fit in with the triangular disposition, reveal a search

for order that is probably indicative of Cézanne's complex and contradictory attitude towards women.

There are echoes of the past in these works, from classical sculpture to Titian and Rubens. Cézanne's profound knowledge of art and literature are assimilated into his conception of an art that represents modern times while retaining the dignity of the great works of the past. His dream of a reconciliation between man and nature stems from his life experience. The bathers were his final meditation on the past, they represent the nostalgia for an idyllic life that belonged to the domain of myth and was yet deeply rooted in the artist's own emotional conflicts. These figures are stripped of all specifics, which accentuates the universal and epic quality of the works, and are placed in an open space to indicate a utopia of freedom and harmony; they bathers stand for the creative power of femininity and can also symbolize the power of imagination. Roger Fry thought these bathers were "the sign of a calculated affront to our notion of feminine beauty," but upon closer consideration we find that, besides anticipating the primitive, sexually assertive women in the early works of Picasso and Matisse, they exert a strange fascination (to which Cézanne has accustomed us) – the fascination of the hermaphrodite and his/her androgynous psychology. The severity and lack of beauty of the bathers makes them psychologically impenetrable.

Then there are the portraits of the old gardener Vallier, which represent Cézanne's lofty spiritual testament. These works integrate the figure into the rhythm of the universe in forms that are the expression of absolute essentiality. Lastly is *Cabanon de Jourdan* – perhaps the last canvas Cézanne worked on before being caught in the fatal thunderstorm. It shows how he succeeded in making the various pictorial elements expressive in and for themselves, while at the same time creating an atmosphere in which those material properties become an integral part of a higher order of nature – thus indicating the fundamental paths that 20th-century art was to take.

240

♦ Still Life, c. 1900.
Oil on canvas,
45.8 × 54.9 cm
(18 × 21 5/8 in).
National Gallery
of Art, Washington,
DC.
The thick dabs
of paint, carefully
constructed
composition and
the colour range
interrupted by
a dash of red, give
the impression
of solidity, an
impression
heightened by the
clearly chiselled
objects, each of which
is an integral part
of a powerfully
structured and
balanced whole.

241

♦ Still Life with Blue Bottle, *c. 1900. Watercolour. Kunsthistorisches Museum, Vienna.* "Cézanne's apples are often rendered with tenderness, especially in the late works," says the critic Meyer Schapiro. *Together with a sugar bowl and a transparent bottle on the simple surface of the table, the fruit is isolated and at the same time enhanced in its austere grandeur.*

242

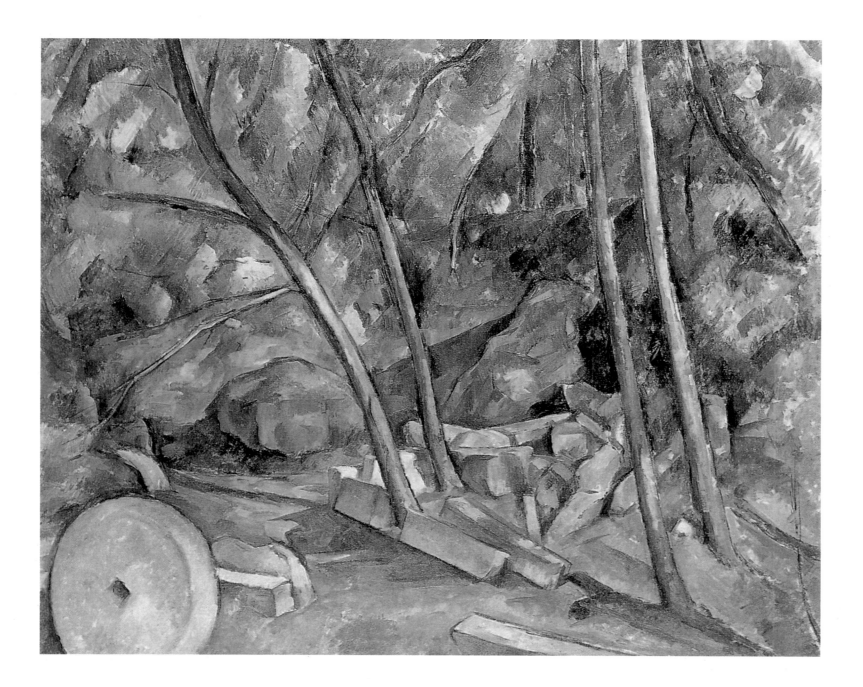

♦ *Opposite:* The Red Rock (Trees and Rocks), c. 1900. *Oil on canvas, 91 × 66 cm (35 7/8 × 26 in). Musée de l'Orangerie, Paris. In the last decades of his production, the character of Cézanne's landscapes changed. He looked for chaotic motifs in which trees and rocks were together in animated, dense settings. The play of light and tonal values create a composition totally lacking in perspective. The vertical rock is an unusual, almost savage element, but it does not disrupt the equilibrium of the composition.*

♦ *Above:* Millstone in the Château Noir Park, 1892-94. *Oil on canvas, 73 × 92 cm (28 × 36 1/4 in). Museum of Art, Philadelphia. An 'indoor' scene in a natural setting, like a cave, without a horizon or an exit, this work represents a wild, romantic site the fascination of which is heightened by its disorder. The colour is a gloomy ensemble of browns, purples, greens and greys – the colours of a sealed off world which nonetheless strives for harmony. A sudden flash of light, as if from a thunderstorm, enhances the modelling of the objects.*

244

♦ *Above:* Pistachio Trees in the Château Noir Courtyard, *c. 1990. Pencil and watercolour, 54 × 43 cm (21 1/4 × 17 in). Art Institute, Chicago.*

♦ *Opposite:* The Balcony, *c, 1900. Pencil and watercolour, 55 × 39 cm (21 5/8 × 15 3/8 in). Museum of Art, Philadelphia.*

247

♦ *Opposite:* Pines and
Rocks at the Château
Noir, *1900. Pencil
and watercolour,
46 × 36 cm
(18 1/8 × 14 1/8 in).
University Art
Museum, Princeton.*

♦ *Above:* Mont Sainte-
Victoire, *1900-1902.
Pencil and
watercolour,
31 × 48 cm
(11 1/2 × 18 7/8 in).
Cabinet des Dessins,
Musée du Louvre,
Paris.*

248

♦ *Above:* Le Château Noir, *1900-1904. Oil on canvas, 73.7 × 96.6 cm (29 × 38 in). National Gallery of Art, Washington, DC. The green patches of the foliage attenuate* the contrast of the *ochre and blue. The sky is animated by the arabesque of the bare branches; in the background is the Mont du Cengle, at left a path leads to the Maison Maria.*

♦ *Opposite:* The Forked Pine Tree *in the Château Noir Park, 1900-1904. Oil on canvas, 90.7 × 71.4 cm (35 3/4 × 28 1/8 in). National Gallery, London.*

250

♦ *Above:* The Sailor, *1904-1905.* *Oil on canvas, 107.4 × 74.5 cm (42 1/4 × 29 3/8 in). National Gallery of Art, Washington, DC. In his portraits of the gardener Vallier, Cézanne also represents old age. This canvas* *has a thick impasto here and there which betrays the artist's dogged creative struggle. There is a grandeur in this picture of an old man immersed in his universe and scrutinized by another old man.*

♦ *Opposite:* Woman in Blue, *1900-1904.* *Oil on canvas, 88.5 × 72 cm (34 7/8 × 28 3/8 in). Hermitage Museum, St. Petersburg. Even though they are not character studies, Cézanne's portraits are inevitably marked* *by an impressive physical presence. "For the artist, seeing is conceiving," he said, "and conceiving is composing." And again: "Painting is optical: the substance of our art lies in what our eyes think."*

252

♦ Still Life with Jug and Sugar Bowl, 1900-1906. Watercolour, 48 × 63 cm (18 7/8 × 24 7/8 in). Kunsthistorisches Museum, Vienna. This watercolour is animated and made sensuous by the luminosity of the uncoloured parts of the paper, which gives the picture a life of its own. A symphony of light tones is accompanied by great formal equilibrium afforded by the colour, which creates full volumes and different values.

♦ Still Life with Apples and Peaches, c. 1905. *Oil on canvas 81.2 × 100.6 cm (32 × 39 5/8 in). National Gallery of Art, Washington, DC. This large canvas is dominated by a profound harmony that establishes its density. There are three dashes of pinkish white: in the jug, the tablecloth and the bowl. The texture is not thick but the execution was certainly slow and carefully thought out.*

254

♦ *Above:* Landscape in Blue, *1904-1906, 102 × 83 cm (40 1/8 × 32 5/8 in). Hermitage Museum, St. Petersburg. Kandinsky said about Cézanne: "It is not a man, an apple or a tree that is represented; Cézanne utilizes everything to create something called a picture, which is the creation of a purely interior, pictorial resonance." Cézanne probably did not finish this canvas, which is an example of the turbulent pictorial handling of his final years.*

♦ *Opposite:* Rocks and Branches at Bibémus, *1900-1904. Oil on canvas, 50 × 61 cm (19 5/8 × 24 in). Musée du Petit Palais, Paris.*

256

♦ Mont Sainte-Victoire Seen from Les Lauves, *1902-1906. Oil on canvas, 65 × 81 cm (25 5/8 × 31 7/8 in). Nelson-Atkins Museum of Art,* *Kansas City. Mont Sainte-Victoire dominates the plain east of Aix-en-Provence and plays an important role in Cézanne's art and personality.* *The artist used the mountain as the motif for a great series of canvases in the last phase of his production. Here it rises up in the distance against a* *cloudy sky, over a vast green plain in which one can make out trees and houses, while the foothills, which are darker, are delimited by a clear-cut line.*

257

♦ Mont Sainte-Victoire, *1902-1906.* *Watercolour,* *31 × 48 cm* *(12 1/4 × 18 7/8 in).* *Museum of Art,* *Philadelphia. "Look* *at Sainte-Victoire.* *What sweep! What* commanding *thirst* *for sunshine! And* *what melancholy in* *the evening when all* *that tension is* *released, abated.* *Those blocks were on* *fire an hour earlier,* *and the fire is still* *in them," Cézanne* *said to Gasquet.* *Set in the midday* *sunlight, the* *mountain, magnetic* *in its massiveness,* *is permeated by* *subtle modulated* *colours that* *transform it into* *an immaterial* *substance. The basic* *elements of the* *landscape are* *underscored by dabs* *of colour that lend a* *miraculous ethereal* *quality to the canvas.*

258

♦ Left: Mont Sainte-Victoire, 1902-1906. Oil on canvas, 65 × 81 cm (25 5/8 × 31 7/8 in). Kunsthaus, Zurich. As one moves away from this canvas, the interlocking multicoloured fragments take on form and move in all directions, lending a sensation of immense space to the work. The individual forms are not important in themselves, but serve to create an overall, more abstract vision. One feels Cézanne's total identification with nature.

♦ Above: Mont Sainte-Victoire Seen from Les Lauves, 1904-1906. Oil on canvas, 60 × 72 cm (23 5/8 × 28 3/8 in). Kunstmuseum, Basle.

♦ Mont Sainte-Victoire Seen from Les Lauves, *1905-1906. Oil on canvas, 60 × 73 cm (23 5/8 × 28 5/8 in). Pushkin Museum, Moscow.*
Some critics feel that the rich textures and sure handling show that this was the last view of the mountain that Cézanne executed at Les Lauves. This canvas is darker than the others, with acid greens mixed with blues and purples, while the middle *is dominated by ochre hues. In 1956 André Masson said that in Cézanne's last period "the concentration is so intense that it explodes. It is a 'future phenomenon.' Tired of offering the richness of his vision to a blind world, Cézanne now speaks only with the interlocutor in his inner self. The result is supreme freedom, that of Beethoven's last quartets and of Zen monks."*

♦ Le Château Noir, 1903-1904. Oil on canvas, 73 × 92 cm (28 3/4 × 36 1/4 in). Museum of Modern Art, New York. This work once belonged to Monet, who is supposed to have said, when showing it to a friend: "Ah, yes! Cézanne is the greatest of us all." Patches of colour in an irregular pattern of brushstrokes, reflect the artist's strong sensations and create a dense surface from which a powerful image emerges.

262

♦ Le Château Noir, c. 1904. Oil on canvas, 73 × 92 cm (28 3/4 × 36 1/4 in). Reinhart Collection, Winterthur. Halfway between Aix and Tholonet, the Château Noir has the strange appearance of a ruin because of the columns of an orangery that was left unfinished. The colour of the buildings is the same as the stone found in the Bibémus quarry. Cézanne here paints the luminous orange facade of the western wing, with the red door dominating the greens of the luxuriant vegetation.

263

♦ Le Château Noir, 1904-1906. Oil on canvas, 70 × 82 cm (27 1/2 × 32 1/4 in). Picasso Collection. The individual parts of this motif are reduced to pictorial elements, patches of colour in an irregular pattern of brushstrokes masterfully arranged so as to mix freely and animate the surface. The seemingly casual unity, the compact structure, and the wealth of nuances produce an image with great inner dynamism, or, as Cézanne himself said, "a harmony parallel to nature."

264

♦ Cabanon de Jourdan, *1906. Oil on canvas, 65 × 81 cm (25 5/8 × 31 7/8 in). Galleria Nazionale d'Arte Moderna, Rome.*
The composition of this work is marked by the clarity of its forms; the space is dominated by the low building in bright ochre under a blue sky. This may be Cézanne's last painting and was *probably executed in the Beauregard area north of Aix. It is an example of the artist's desire to lend the greatest body and depth to objects and at the same time integrate them into an all-embracing cosmic life, according to his vision of the flux and permanence of matter in a superior order of nature.*

◀ Large Bathers, 1894-1905. Oil on canvas, 130 × 195 cm (51 1/8 × 76 3/4 in). National Gallery, London. One of the three versions of the large-scale canvases of female bathers. The elemental figures are a sort of challenge to aesthetic canons in the name of modernity, and at the same time stem from the great examples of the past.

The bathers canvases, which worked a tremendous influence on modern art, have often been related to Cézanne's desire to "redo Poussin after nature." The Old Masters were a constant source of inspiration for him, but he always felt that artistic intelligence without a study of nature was of no value.

266

♦ Female Bathers,
1900-1905.
*Oil on canvas,
51.3 × 61.7 cm
(20 1/8 × 24 1/4 in).
Art Institute,
Chicago. Summarily
sketched groups of
figures lie in the
midst of a landscape
that is rendered with
luminous, liquid
brushstrokes.
Here Cézanne was
experimenting* *with space and
composition, and
was to find the
solution in the three
versions of* Large
Bathers *– at the
National Gallery
of London, Barnes
Foundation, and
Philadelphia
Museum of Art – that
represent his final
meditation on the
theme of the nude
in a natural setting.*

♦ Large Bathers, 1906. Oil on canvas, 208 × 249 cm (81 7/8 × 98 in). Museum of Art, Philadelphia. In a frieze-like arrangement, the figures are modelled by means of warm and cold tonal contrasts. The forms are enveloped in a diffused luminosity that is suggested by the tonal modulations on the bodies. There are patches of whitish ground that create spaces in which the colour vibrates, saturated by the neighbouring hues. Colour delimits the forms and sets them in relief. Cézanne paints the areas closest to the spectator in light tones, so that those further from our eye seem to become darker. The complexity of this work, while being carefully planned, reflects the artist's profound existential experience.

BIBLIOGRAPHY

AA.VV., *Cézanne e le avanguardie*, edited by N. Ponente, Rome 1981
G. ADRIANI, *Paul Cézanne. Der Liebeskampf*, Munich 1980
A. BARNES and V. DE MAZIA, *The Art of Cézanne*, New York 1939
É. BERNARD, *Souvenirs sur Paul Cézanne*, Paris 1921
A. BERTRAM, *Cézanne*, London 1929
L. BRION GUERRY, *Cézanne et l'expression de l'espace*, Paris 1950, II ed. 1966
Cézanne, catalogue, Pavillon Vendôme, Aix-en-Provence; preface by F. Novotny, 1956
Cézanne, catalogue, Österreichische Galerie, Vienna; preface by F. Novotny, 1961
Cézanne and Structure in Modern Painting, catalogue, The Solomon R. Guggenheim Museum, New York 1963
Cézanne dans les Musées Nationaux, catalogue, Orangerie des Tuileries, Paris; introduction by H. Adhemar; catalogue edited by M. Hoog assisted by S. Rufenacht and G. Monnier, 1974
Cézanne les années de jeunesse 1859-1872, catalogue, Musée d'Orsay, Paris; Royal Academy, London; National Gallery of Art, Washington; introduction by J. Rewald; articles by L. Gowing, M.L. Krumrine, M. Tompkins Lewis, S. Patin; catalogue edited by L. Gowing, 1988-89
Cézanne. Les dernières années (1895-1906), catalogue, Grand Palais, Paris; introduction by W. Rubin; articles by L. Brion Guerry, J. Rewald, G. Monnier, 1978
Cézanne. Paintings, catalogue, The Tate Gallery, London; edited by L. Gowing, 1954
Cézanne. Paintings, Watercolors and Drawings. A Loan Exhibition, catalogue, The Art Institute, Chicago; The Metropolitan Museum of Art, New York; preface by D. Catton; introduction by T. Rousseau jr., 1952
Cézanne. The Bathers, catalogue, Kunstmuseum, Basle; edited by C. Geelhaar, M.L. Krumrine, 1989
A. CHAPPUIS, *The Drawings of Paul Cézanne. A Catalogue Raisonné*, 2 vols., London 1973
R. COGNIAT, *Cézanne*, Paris 1939
G. COQUIOT, *Cézanne*, Paris 1919
B. DORIVAL, *Cézanne*, Paris 1948
E. D'ORS, *Paul Cézanne*, Paris 1930
H. DÜCHTING, *Paul Cézanne 1831-1906. Nature into Art*, Cologne 1990
F. ELGAR, *Cézanne*, New York 1975
E. FAURE, *Paul Cézanne*, Paris 1926
P.H. FEIST, *Paul Cézanne*, Leipzig 1963
R. FRY, *Cézanne. A Study of His Development*, New York 1927
J. GASQUET, *Cézanne. A Memoir with a Conversation*, London 1991
L. GOWING, *Paul Cézanne. The Basel Sketchbooks*, New York 1988
Hommage à Cézanne, catalogue, Orangerie des Tuileries, Paris; introduction by G. Bazin; catalogue edited by A. Châtelet, 1954
Hommage à Paul Cézanne, catalogue, Wildenstein & Co., London; preface by J. Rewald, 1939
M. HOOG, *Cézanne – Father of the 20th-Century Art*, New York 1994
R. HUYGHE, *Cézanne*, Paris 1936
R. JEAN, *Cézanne, la vie, l'espace*, Paris 1986
G. JEDLICKA, *Cézanne*, Bern 1948
F. JOURDAIN, *Cézanne*, Paris - New York 1950
L. LARGUIER, *Le Dimanche avec Paul Cézanne: souvenirs*, Paris 1925
L'opera completa di Cézanne, edited by A. Gatto and S. Orienti, Milan 1970
G. MACK, *Paul Cézanne*, New York 1935, II ed. 1936
J. MEIER-GRAEFE, *Paul Cézanne*, Munich 1910, II ed. 1918
S. MONNERET, *Cézanne, Zola. La fraternité du génie*, Paris 1978
J.E. MULLER, *Cézanne*, Paris 1982
R.W. MURPHY, *The World of Cézanne*, New York 1968
R.J. NIESS, *Cézanne, Zola and Manet*, Ann Arbor 1968
F. NOVOTNY, *Cézanne*, London 1961
Paul Cézanne. Correspondance, publiée par J. Rewald, Paris 1937
Paul Cézanne. Letters, edited by J. Rewald, London 1941
G. PLAZY, *Cézanne ou la peinture absolue*, Paris 1988
N. PONENTE, *Cézanne*, Bologna 1980
M. RAYNAL, *Cézanne*, Geneva - Paris - New York 1954
J. REWALD, *Cézanne. A Biography*, New York - Paris 1986
J. REWALD, *Cézanne: The Watercolors*, Boston - London 1983
R.M. RILKE, *Lettres sur Cézanne*, Paris 1944
G. RIVIÈRE, *Cézanne le peintre solitaire*, Paris 1933, II ed. 1936
G. RIVIÈRE, *Le Maître Paul Cézanne*, Paris 1923
Sainte-Victorie, Cézanne, catalogue, Musée Granet, Musée des Tapisseries, Pavillon de Vendôme, Aix-en-Provence; edited by D. Coutagne, B. Ely, 1990
M. SCHAPIRO, *Cézanne*, New York 1952
R. SCHIFF, *Cézanne and the End of the Impressionism*, Chicago 1984
L. VENTURI, *Cézanne. Watercolours*, London 1943
L. VENTURI, *Cézanne, son art, son œuvre*, 2 vols., Paris 1936
L. VENTURI, *Cézanne*, Geneva 1978
R. VERDI, *Cézanne*, London 1992
A. VOLLARD, *Paul Cézanne. His Life and Art*, New York 1937
A. VOLLARD, *Paul Cézanne*, Paris 1914, II ed. 1919

INDEX

*Page numbers in roman refer to the text,
those in italic to the captions,
those in bold to the colour plates.*